the EastOver Anthology *of*
Rural Stories

WRITERS OF COLOR

2023

Keith Pilapil Lesmeister, editor

THE EASTOVER ANTHOLOGY OF RURAL STORIES

WRITERS OF COLOR – 2023

Keith Pilapil Lesmeister, editor

ISBN 978-1-958094-25-9

FICTION
ANTHOLOGY

BOOK & COVER DESIGN ➜ EK LARKEN

COVER IMAGE ⬅ PAMELASPHOTOPOETRY (iStock)

EastOver Press encourages the use of our publications in educational settings. For questions about educational discounts, contact us online:. www.EastOverPress.com *or* info@EastOverPress.com

PUBLISHED IN THE UNITED STATES OF AMERICA BY

EASTOVER
— PRESS —
Rochester, Massachusetts
www.EastOverPress.com

Rural Stories

WRITERS OF COLOR

CONTENTS

INTRODUCTION

IT'S DIFFICULT TO PINPOINT THE EXACT GENESIS OF this project, this anthology, this collection of short fiction you now hold in your hand. Most of my ideas—at least the ones worth pursuing—come to me while hiking narrow dirt paths around tree-lined bluffs that encase the town in which I live, and this anthology was no different. You've probably gathered, given the description above, that the area is rural. It is. A town of less than ten thousand people, tucked in the far corner of northeast Iowa, a place where the idea of a rural identity extends far beyond conversations, editorials, podcasts, and cable news. From my home, Madison is three hours to the east, Iowa City three hours to the south, and the Twin Cities three hours to the north.

People living in communities like mine aren't simply thinking about the urban-rural divide, we're living it. Politics plays an outsized role in our lives now. Pundits, political pollsters, politicians themselves all want to better understand why the county directly to the west of where I live went 20+ points for the Democratic candidate in 2012 and 20+ points for the Republican candidate in 2016. That forty-point swing attracted all the major news outlets, most recently *Meet the Press*. People want to know *why*. What's going on out here in the sticks? What's important to the rural folks? What do we have foremost on our minds?

And while I believe this isn't an anthology about American politics, it is a book overtly geared toward political issues ranging from issues of race, sexuality and gender identity, failed government policies about a mysterious outbreak, and an inequitable health system. These subjects may feel expected, but these stories subvert, surprise, and complicate our ideas and expectations. They make no attempt at easy answers. Instead, they focus squarely on the characters who inhabit the stories, allowing readers an opportunity to imagine for a moment the life of someone in a situation perhaps far different from the one they live. This is the beauty of fiction. It offers nuance and complexity, and steers clear of empty promises or attempts at easy answers. Frankly, I wouldn't trust anyone who offered simple answers to complex questions that might take years to understand, if ever. No amount of writing or explaining or pontificating or dividing or name-calling will help understand the nuance and texture that encapsulates those of us who live in rural spaces—those of us who co-exist more or less in harmony despite not always seeing eye-to-eye on every major issue, political or otherwise.

Jamie Figueroa writes about a woman whose "remission ended" and whose backyard is inundated with rabbits. Risë Kevalshar Collins's story revolves around Black siblings who navigate parts of northern Idaho before finally being pulled over by a police officer. Libby Flores features a man who spies on his terminally ill wife in the strawberry fields of California. Jennifer Morales's protagonist is a blue-collar man from a small town who has become obsessed with a performance artist he has met in Milwaukee. He now finds excuses to leave his small Wisconsin town to return to the city in hopes of finding her.

Throughout these eleven stories, you'll find tragedy and heartbreak, failure and infidelity, pain and loss. But always, too, lingering in the far-off corners, you'll find a flourishing humanity, humor and hope, and a *not-going-to-give-up* attitude from an array of compelling characters living and existing—not always thriving, but always trying—in the rich tapestry of rural spaces.

Once again, this book doesn't promise answers, but it does promise engagement, new perspectives, and more than anything it offers a pure and thoughtful glimpse into the lives of rural characters. My hope is that you finish these stories as I did—not with so-called answers, but with a clearer and richer understanding of who our neighbors are, what they value, and our intricate and closely-held connections.

—KEITH PILAPIL LESMEISTER, *editor*

⤛

The Lesser Light of Dying Stars

Jinwoo Chong

T IS BELIEVED THAT MR. LEON LEVITT OF PERIDOT, Arizona, began to emit sometime around his forty-third birthday—"emit" being the retroactive clinical term ascribed by those of the science community studying SDR phenomena where they occur. Given the location of the Levitts' home in a topographical trough flooded with natural light, it is likely that Mr. Levitt's condition was, at first, imperceptible to both himself and Nora, his wife of eight years. While total light emittance can stay negligible for weeks, radiologists argue that, in theory, within an enclosed room with no windows, some may have perceived certain physical changes (paler skin, a subtle translucence to the irises and hair). The difference would have been, for most, slight. As has been observed, Leon Levitt was emitting for some time before his skin began, visibly, to glow. On that day, Nora woke in bed, especially dazed, and realized that the soft blue light that had alerted her eyes to a new day was not the sun, which had not yet risen, but the sleeping form of her husband, lighting their creased linens from underneath like luna moth wings curled about their bodies.

Sub-dermal radiative phenomena are so named for the origin of emitted light from beneath the skin. Mid- to late-stage novas often emit a light so intense that bones, surgical implants, and major blood vessels can be seen with stunning definition, similar to holding a powerful flashlight against one's arm. Leon Levitt was admitted to San Carlos Apache Healthcare Corporation that morning, attracting a crowd of attending doctors in triage when eyes fell for the first time on his luminous body. Hours later, South Korean media reported a second emergence in a secluded hamlet of Gyeongju: five-year-old nova Bek Ki-Jung, whose parents had brought her to the emergency room after they noticed her bathtub suds begin to gleam around her as she played. Both Ki-Jung and Mr. Levitt were early-stage SDR, diffusing roughly the same brightness as a fluorescent lightbulb. Sonoya Merrick, head of San Carlos' Radiology Group, noted in the Levitts' log a postscript to her examination: *whatever words there are to better illustrate—they are beyond my degrees.*

It was on the same day that the media descended in Peridot that Saul and Priya Morrow of Jordan, Minnesota, lost their son, eighteen-year-old Jack, in a car crash that had left two friends in intensive care and three pedestrians dead on a neighboring crosswalk. The accident made the papers in Minneapolis, but most had larger matters on their minds after the glowing man of Arizona had captured national attention, the little Korean girl following soon after. A celebrity medical figurehead had already claimed on air that the two emergences were linked and that more would arise, predictably around cell towers, natural gas processing plants, and the like. Saul and his wife received this news blindly, for they were burying their son.

Jack Morrow's injuries had been explicated in detail by the coroner, an insistence of his mother's after they were advised— strongly—not to view the body before embalming. The car had dipped slightly over the curb at forty miles an hour, jamming its front axis, launching into a roll that crushed its roof against the side of a nearby crafts store. The top of Jack's skull had been lopped off by bent metal; broken windshield glass had severed his nose and ears. He had died in the brief amount of time it had taken for his lungs to collapse. Fortunate, the coroner said. Priya had raised her head, ablaze upon hearing the word, but did not speak. She gave a lasting look to the wall, behind it the empty room where her son lay.

Saul Morrow squeezed his wife's hand. The coroner had finished his report and was waiting for them to leave his office. The little television in the reception area outside was blaring an account by a neighbor of the Levitts. Priya listened, only vaguely. The embalmers could reconstruct Jack's nose and ears in time for a funeral service next week. Jack's grandparents needed to be told, as well as the parents of Jack's two friends—two boys he'd known since preschool. She looked at Saul, at a space beyond his eyes, and smiled. Saul would recount later how that little curve of his wife's lips had, for just a brief moment, righted their tilting planet, though she would not remember it that way, nor would she remember smiling at all, for what was there really to smile about, anymore?

They went home that afternoon to their other son, sixteen- year-old David, who had not been allowed to go to the morgue and had waited an hour for their return. Saul placed a hand on his youngest's shoulder. They stood apart, unsupported, the three of them still as granite pillars on their aged blue lawn. David waited for his father to speak. After a minute of silence, they walked together into the house.

In Busan, doctors placed Bek Ki-Jung under strict observation. A sociable girl who was known to often spin far-flung stories at bedtime to the amusement of her parents, Ki-Jung remained jovial amid her new surroundings, asking after friends and school assignments. The emergence of her light had been seized upon by clergy of the Shincheonji Church of Jesus, intent on proving the girl's luminous skin a miracle from God. Within the week, six cases had emerged in Africa, twelve more in the Americas, and eighteen combined in Europe and Asia, the majority of which were co-opted by various religious groups and sects as similar divine acts. Ki-Jung pointed to a photograph of herself that appeared one evening on television, saying nothing. Her mother, Ki-Won, requested the cable disconnected.

In Peridot, it was noted that Leon Levitt, a private wealth manager and father of twin eight-year-old girls, appeared in high spirits, inviting attention from press and visiting doctors as his body brightened. He quipped to reporters that he expected a check for reducing the hospital's electric bill; his presence in a darkened room now tended to give the appearance of the space being lit by stage lights. His pearly white skin had begun to obscure details of his face. Only film calibrated to the lowest levels of exposure could accurately capture his image. Nora Levitt, taken to sleeping alongside him on a pull-out bed, eventually relocated at his insistence to a hotel across the street, where she and their girls could look out the window and see the corner suite on the eighth-floor flash in the night behind shades pulled futilely across.

A UN-appointed council of the world's leading radiologists had been assembled to study the emergences. It had become clear that Mr. Levitt and others were not expected to darken anytime soon, that their bodies were brightening at an exponential pace, increasing anywhere from a hundred to several thousand lumens a day. Teams assembled a working knowledge of the phenomena in anticipation of treatment options. In several cases around the globe, light emittance alerted doctors to previously undiscovered tumors in organs like the esophagus or liver that blotted dark under the skin. In Nigeria, a ninety-eight-year-old nova died of natural causes while mid-stage, her light ceasing and her skin returning to normal pigment after the moment of her last breath. In Mumbai, an expectant mother's temperature rose around her cervix five weeks into pregnancy; her unborn nova child's heart had started to beat.

After another month, Leon Levitt and a handful of mid-stage novas now too bright to be observed by the naked eye without retina damage were moved to a secure facility in the Great Basin for observation at the insistence of the federal government. Emitting about seven-hundred-fifty-thousand lumens, Mr. Levitt was now roughly the brightness of a single-strobe camera flash, the brightest of the American cases. The team observing him wore polarized goggles in his presence; he engaged their black portals instead of eyes throughout the day. Nora spoke to him nightly through an ultraviolet camera feed; they were making every effort to maintain normalcy in their twin girls' lives. Still, he could not explain to them when he would be back. Their faces, blank and washed of color on his laptop screen, kept him awake far into the night. In Henan, China, a family of five all began emitting within days of each other, feeding rumors of the phenomenon's heritability. With the UN's failures thus far to triangulate a cure, demands rose for protective measures. Dr. Merrick, who had accompanied Mr. Levitt and the others to the Great Basin, found herself on television every other day, emphasizing that SDR phenomena remained entirely manageable with the proper equipment. Her doubts, she expressed to no one.

Within months, Bek Ki-Jung's accelerated SDR had made her the brightest known nova in existence. Her body, emitting a total one million lumens, could be seen from the window of Busan National University Hospital from a distance of up to fifteen miles. Government officials debated her removal from the city; her light had recently begun to attract nightly throngs of religious onlookers. Allowed only limited contact with her parents, Ki-Jung had withdrawn into herself, prone now to bursts of irritability and silence. Ki-Won was the only person in the room that morning, clothed in lead garments and a modified welding mask, when she heard a voice. Ki-Won thought it sounded like *umma*, the girl's first word, a sound that, until recently, had roused her from sleep every morning and bade her goodnight with the sun. Ki-Won sat up from her chair, feeling blindly around, and called her daughter's name. With the mask over her face and heavy polarized glass over the visor, she discerned only blunt shapes.

Later, Ki-Won would recall the slightest vibration in her lead suit, as though she were standing on a bed of sound that travelled up her bones. She reached out a hand to where her daughter lay. Jumped, when the white haze around her seemed to shimmer— she would describe it, in her limited English, as *sparkling*— then all at once, went out. Ki-Won started at the sudden blackness inside her helmet, falling to the floor. She was wrestled from the room by disembodied hands amid shouts. She managed to wrench her helmet off, blinking, stunned, at the newfound dark, and had just enough time to glimpse, over the shoulder of an attending doctor, the charred bed in the center of the room.

Saul Morrow was beset by routine that night. He had taken, in the month after Jack's death, to wandering the house with bare feet, mapping creaks of the old foundation under his toes. Jordan was a small town an hour's drive from the state university where Saul ran a branch of undergraduate admissions. Jack and several of his classmates had expected to enroll that fall. He and Priya had raised both boys here, never giving much thought to moving until about six years ago, entertaining for the span of a week a move to Seattle, a teaching position that Saul eventually turned down. He'd returned to the university two weeks after Jack's funeral and had been received by his colleagues with excruciating solemnity. He was all right, he insisted daily, shrinking their eyes to pinpoints in his mind. The night of Bek Ki-Jung's sublimation, he heard David's footsteps on the stairs behind him. His son wandered slowly into view, holding his phone.

"There's some little girl, in Korea—" He stepped closer. "Just watch this."

A screen slid in front of his eyes. Rolling text under a talking head at the Busan National Hospital explained that the Korean government was scrambling to contain a media storm over what appeared to be the death of the Bek girl the previous morning.

"They disappear," David supplied, when Saul had

said nothing. The video looped, playing again. "The novas. They're saying they disappear."

Saul had not detected much of a change in David's attitudes since Jack's death, save for the way he'd begun to linger after their meals. He was avoiding his room, still furnished with two beds, Jack's side of the walls covered with sun-bleached posters and bulletins; they had shared a room since they were little boys. In those moments—in David's pale, smoothed face—he beheld both sons, who had always looked like twins. He had admired the ease David and Jack had about each other, though the thought filled him now with the weight of sand.

"Mom's sleeping."

David had read his thoughts. Priya had retreated upstairs after their silent dinner without saying goodnight. Saul tried to think of something to say, coming too late. David had already turned and gone the way he'd come, back to his room. Saul paced the rest of the house. He thought about quitting his job. They had savings enough to pay David's tuition, wherever he wished, a luxury that had been afforded them by Jack's death. Saul wondered when it would not pain him to think so logically. He mounted the stairs, turning off to the first door on the right, spying David and Jack's room at the end of the hall. In the dark, he made out her form among the blankets, fumbling with his clothes. She was awake—he could tell by the rigid hunch of her shoulders.

"Priya."

She didn't answer. Saul slid into bed beside her.

Not after he lay there awake for at least an hour did he notice the house was silent that night; David snored loudly when he slept.

The next week, a second and third nova, a husband and wife, sublimated within seconds of each other in a Pennsylvania mill town; their house, lit from every window with brilliant white light, had been set aflame by the event, and burned for half an hour before fire-fighters arrived. The next day, the UN announced plans for a registry; now assumed to expire within the near future, those affected would be able to apply for funds in a manner similar to life insurance. The registry required a death certificate to issue payments, igniting outrage around the world: who was to say any of the novas were really dead? Religious groups theorized a process akin to the biblical rapture, though disagreements among faiths and a lack of evidence in either direction did not move conversations beyond conspiracy. Several novas emerged in protest, refusing to be sent to the Great Basin and other facilities. State legislation could not move fast enough to evict them lawfully before they, too, sublimated. A more practical solution emerged, shuttled by an unexpected spokesman: the Spanish shipping baron, King Terzian II. A controversial figure in Europe and personal friend to the ruler of Bahrain, among others, Terzian and his businesses had been the subject of a number of inquiries by the World Court in the previous decade. Nursing a bruised reputation, he had emerged back in the public eye to address a crowd of hundreds from the steps of Madrid's City Council one month after Bek Ki-Jung's sublimation. The world as it was, he explained, could not address the issue of SDR phenomena as long as the bureaucracy surrounding the UN council remained intact. There were options, he insisted, that lacked the conclusive efficacy for governments to risk investment. He paused, gazing down at his hands. "My wife," he said, and nothing more for several moments.

He mentioned with disdain the efforts of certain governments to contain the phenomenon strictly for observation, the Great Basin facility in the United States housing at least four hundred novas since Leon Levitt's arrival there. Within a month's time, he vowed, the jewel of his business empire, a sprawling Cartagena shipyard, would be converted into a commune for the affected. He had amassed an international team of doctors and flown them there to begin their research. As volunteers, afflicted persons could elect for radiation, experimental gene editing, and stem cell procedures—solutions bound by red tape as pharmaceutical firms buckled under the floundering market. The news, and the impending dissolution of Terzian's businesses, sent shockwaves. Many sought to prove the plan a bluff. Terzian's third wife, mother to his eighth and ninth children, had rarely been seen in the public eye. The stage of her condition was, as of yet, unknown. But within a month, the businessman had kept his word. The Spanish commune, an investment of billions of euros, had become the headiest option for novas seeking treatment. Hundreds arrived in Cartagena, flown together in packs by refurbished cargo freighters if their light had grown too harsh for commercial air. Papers asked every week: was this the fate that awaited all humanity? Not for a century, if trends were sustained, news that nevertheless fell on deaf ears as more woke to thin blue light in their bedrooms, and more, still, burned out around the world.

Nora Levitt received a call in the morning. Dr. Merrick relayed the news with as much tact as she could muster over the phone. She packed a bag, alerted her sister across town that the girls would be home from school that afternoon, and got into the car that arrived an hour later. She'd begged Leon to consider Spain.

He was too far along to pique the government's interest or resources anymore. Neither he nor Nora believed in a cure, too afraid of what would happen if they indulged in fantasy. Nora had argued he would be happier there, free to roam, to take the long walks to which he had accustomed himself back in Peridot. They had spoken often of a trip to Europe, for the girls. Leon had refused, or so she thought; he did not speak much anymore. Thus he had chosen confinement, a view of the red deserts of his childhood through his plate glass window. Nora was told that he complained more often of fatigue. The ultraviolet cameras captured his form reclined on his aluminum bed for nearly twenty hours a day. Armed guards escorted her through the facility, emptier than usual. Hundreds had abounded for the commune.

She was padlocked into a lead suit, fitted for a helmet, and shown behind an iron door. The light flooded her visor, strong enough despite the polarized glass to make her squint. Still, in the dark haze she could make out a shape, a man she knew. She stepped carefully toward him. She felt the heat that she had been warned about. Her husband shone in front of her, baking her outsides; she recalled the feeling of laying out with the girls at their favorite pool back home. Leon asked about them, she told him they knew, they had known for weeks ever since the Bek girl; she could not stop them hearing it at school. His grip on her hands through the rubber gloves was only a faint pressure. He'd reached out, nervously, swatting the air. It struck Nora that he could no longer see her. He told her he felt faint and had been so for the past day. She raised a hand.

"Nora?"

She felt in her bones a vibration, up through the floor, in her hand as she felt around his face. She made her choice.

"It's all right."

Her fingers closed around the bolt that locked her helmet into place. The door was open, several people shouting behind her as they scrambled, encumbered in their suits, to stop her.

"It's all right."

She lifted the bulky ironwork off. She looked at him, smiled. For two, three seconds she stood bathed in light that swarmed, pulsing the air, a moment longer, then shrank to nothing, plunging the room into blackness. An attending doctor was the first to reach her: she turned slowly on the spot toward their voices, the trace of a curl on her lips.

Saul Morrow, pacing around the kitchen, turned the corner and found David in the doorway, hands out as though feeling through space by touch. They looked at each other, unnatural as it was for both to be awake so early in the morning. Saul opened his mouth to offer breakfast—chopped bacon and fried eggs together in a pan, his son's favorite—and when his eyes caught the light, a seeping blue under the boy's skin that darkened around his eyes and under his fingernails, he thought for a moment of his luck: the godsend to fathers able to look on their sons as if for the first time.

David thought he knew what he wanted. More asylum seekers were pouring into the Spanish commune every day. A photograph had been taken from the International Space Station, a nickel-sized flare of white light on Earth's surface, now the brightest spot on the planet.

"I'm a danger here. What if I burn the house down? They said the Korean girl's mother only lived because of the suit she had on. There's real treatment in Spain. They're taking bigger risks there."

He almost stopped himself saying it, as if forbidden: "What if they can cure me?"

He grew hot, the way boys did when they could tell their fathers weren't listening.

"Why can't you see this is what I want?" David filled his lungs, and his father could swear his skin brightened several degrees as he did so. How long had it been? Days? Weeks? He had failed to notice.

"Dad."

"You're not going."

"Dad—"

Saul took two steps to where he stood. Any day now David would realize his own body had eclipsed his father's. When that happened he would, for the first time, picture Saul's death, the wilting of joints and papering of the skin. It would make him gentler, kinder. It had been the same with Jack, a week shy of his high school graduation when he died. Saul remembered their last words: the trash had been left in the garage and had missed the trucks that morning. Jack had apologized, placing his hands, folded earnestly into each other, at his waist, and his sincerity had so shaken both Saul and Priya that their annoyance had crumbled instantly. There it was, there he was, at the end of their line—David blinked his eyes, dragging his arm across his face with impatience. He was so young and trying not to be.

"If—If I'm going to—"

Out of pride, or some other stupid, boyish determination, he did not reach out for his father.

"You'd be able to visit me," he tried, feebly, lowering his head.

Saul held his breath, afraid for a moment that he'd be left there in the kitchen for the rest of the day. He raised his hands, had to wait only a moment before David relented, leaning forward to rest his head in the crook of his father's neck, and his light threw a ghost's shapes on the walls.

Nora Levitt would not see again, that was certain; her face had begun to swell just minutes after exposure. Dr. Merrick did not see much gore in her line of work but the sight of it had turned her stomach. They operated quickly, given the inflammation; with luck, the skin would heal on its own. Had it been worth it, Dr. Merrick wondered, as her breath caught; the helicopter had taken off, en route with her team back to Peridot. She stopped herself; it was not her place to conspire, with her own family at home, safe. Her husband had called the day before: a girl in their daughter's class had withdrawn from school. She longed for them both while recalling Nora's calm, listening patiently to paramedics as they wheeled her from the dark room. That had been the image marked ink-like on Dr. Merrick's mind—the serenity, the empty smile on her lips as she turned from the spot where Leon had stood.

Hundreds more had rejected the Spanish commune and its copy facilities. Everywhere, they burned out. Sublimations depleted municipal resources and resulted in countless injuries, charred remains of homes and hospices, dead caregivers and relatives. In Spain, no solutions had emerged in almost a year. Data on late-stage SDR was scarce; few instruments could withstand the massive heat expulsion. Various governments, under pressure from citizen's advocacy groups, revisited the option of federal laws to mandate eviction. A tragedy occurred in Geyongju—the brightening of Bek Ki-Won, who had lost her daughter a year earlier. The event, occurring in the night, was the fastest on record at only a matter of seconds and had left her husband with third-degree burns to the right side of his face and body. He died twelve days later in isolated care.

David took his meals in his room, reheated takeout, fast food, things Saul brought home from the grocery store after work. They had been eating like this since Jack's funeral, food only a sustenance. David's light had become too harsh to let him roam the house. At dinner time, he waited with the door closed for Saul to set his food in the hallway. Then, for several brief and searing moments, the house would go white as he emerged. Saul closed his eyes around the corner of the second-floor landing, feeling his skin bake, waited for the comforting darkness to return, his blood beating against the surface of his skin, as David shut his door.

It had changed within the year. Eurasia logged less than ten emergences in the last month. Numbers at the Spanish commune and others around the world had dwindled to bare occupancies; novas were expiring faster than new ones could emerge. With fewer and fewer patients, much of the science community had, for better or worse, abandoned treatment efforts. Saul had relayed this information to David one afternoon through the bedroom door. He was one of the only ones left. Saul had said it like that, as though proud. David was quieter than normal that day.

"Hungry?"

David made a noise. Saul listened for more, hearing none. "Why don't we eat out here with you?" he said, "I think your mother would like that. We can talk through the door."

The massive initiatives undertaken by governments to sequester the novas were being cut their funding. Saul had read an essay by a Dr. Merrick of the Great Basin facility: what was to stop the phenomena from emerging again, in even greater numbers? It seemed a question nobody cared to answer, thankful for the darkness in their neighborhoods and cities, and the stars in their places on the black ribbon of the sky. Saul gripped a flyer in his hand, something he'd found this morning and had been saving to share with David for the past few hours. He thought desperately of lifting his son's mood, knowing it would only be for a moment and reaching, anyway, for it. David had turned seventeen the month before, with a cake left in front of his bedroom door and a scarce handful of calls that Saul held just under the door on speaker. David had so many friends. Most of them, Saul reasoned, still had their own fear to contend with.

"I found something here," he began, "Those visors, that would let me see you. They cost a fortune but maybe if… if you'd like—"

"Dad."

The sun had begun to dip low over the trees, spilling gold flames through the dark branches. Down the hall, Saul heard his wife get up from their bed and run the sink.

"It's dark." David's voice had dropped to a whisper. Saul moved closer, the wedge of light under the door was lengthening as the sky blackened. "All over, in here. I can't see. I haven't for—couple days."

He said no more. Saul pressed his ear to the door, closing his eyes. Carefully, he stepped away. "I'll be back," he said, "I'll be right back, David."

He turned down the hall, screwing his fists savagely into his eyes, breathing once, twice, then again until the feeling it would never stop had stopped. Quietly, he entered their bedroom. Priya was gazing over the sink at her face in the mirror. He thought for a moment about her silence all these months, expecting anger. It would not come. Their eyes met—the last time they had, he couldn't remember.

"Let's eat in the hallway tonight," he said at last. "I think we'd all like that."

Priya looked a few seconds longer at him. She dried her hands. She had thinned considerably; they both had. When at last she said it, her voice rung like tolling bells, demanding he listen, and he remarked to himself that it was one of the reasons he had not yet forgotten, why he loved her.

"I don't remember his face. Either of them."

Saul tightened his mouth against his teeth. He tried to imagine the way David's hair fell in ocean's crests about his head, arms exploding violently from stocky shoulders, stockier than either him or Jack. His rocky hands, he didn't know when they had become so rough—

"If I could just see him."

It was neither question nor answer. Saul reached his hands up, rubbed his face dry. This was what it felt like to breathe clearly, to know. He came to her in the bathroom, bringing her hands to his face. They stood there for minutes. Then they turned around, back to the hall lit with a sliver of blinding light under David's door. Priya sensed, reaching it, the slightest tremor in the floorboards, working its way up her knees and unsound spine to the tips of her fingers. She held her husband's hand tight in hers, she reached the other out to take hold of the doorknob, warm to the touch. "David?" She turned it, opened the door. They walked inside.

≺

White Bird
Risë Kevalshar Collins

for John Robert Lewis

REMA DRIVES HER TWO BRINDLE BULLMASTIFFS, her younger sibling whom she calls Brother, and his veridian-eyed part Maine Coon cat through Idaho. Idaho: famous for potatoes and hate groups. They are traveling from north to south to the capital, Boise—a politically blue city, in a purple county, in a blood-red state.

This is the first time Prema and Brother have ventured so far south along Highway 95, past star garnet mines and syringa flowers, through Palouse prairies and undulating hills. The road rushes before them like water. A single woman, she's grateful her ten-year-old silver SUV is paid for and runs well. Under her hands, the gray leather of the steering wheel is smooth and smells faintly of Persian rose lotion. Mama loved roses.

When she cleared out her office last week, she took Brother's elegant painting of Mama off the wall. For months there'd been talk about the mental health programs being eliminated due to budget cuts, and then that day came. She removed her license from above her desk and packed the painting of Mama, protectress, wearing a flowing blue taffeta dress, smiling as she played a piano adorned with a vase of English roses. Prema inherited Mama's intuition, perseverance, and capable artistic hands.

After working three years in Bonners Ferry and two years in St. Maries, she's seen that the longer someone is stuck in North Idaho without work, the harder it is to leave. Some never do. She knows she and Brother must get out by October or else they will be trapped for ten months—summer through winter—without income.

They have three months to find an affordable larger city, one with good work opportunities for Brother, an unemployed artist who didn't finish school after being bullied by a professor. To survive, he's sporadically worked as an administrative assistant. The new city must have a university so Prema can return to school to earn a third degree. Her motto: *A modern woman needs a degree. A woman of color needs two. A black woman needs three.* They want a city near a military base so there's some possibility of diversity, a city that's animal friendly and, hopefully, people friendly. They have three months.

Southern-born, they'd thought of relocating to Charleston. But not long ago in Charleston, a twenty-one-year-old male white supremacist shot and murdered nine black people in a Christian church. They vetoed a possible move to Chapel Hill where, months prior, three Muslim students had been shot and killed by their white male neighbor over a disputed parking space. They ruled out the artistic city of Asheville for being, like Chapel Hill, in a state christened *Klansville, USA* due to its history of ten thousand members.

When Prema was called to interview in Bozeman, Brother—a prima donna afraid of dying in the cold—refused to go. Though friends promised *Bozeman cold feels warmer than Idaho cold because it's a dry cold*, he was unconvinced.

Sandpoint was too small, few jobs. Coeur d'Alene, too expensive. Moscow offered the university—only. Lewiston was ugly due to its bleak landscape and, thanks to the Potlach paper mill, it stank. They traveled to Santa Fe, were drawn to the Native Americans, land, sky, art, but blacks made up only about one percent of the population, job opportunities seemed sparse and the move would be too costly. They'd come to realize that Boulder, a charming college town, was affordable only to the rich—but, for them, a pipe dream.

Prema researched Boise. She queried coworkers who'd lived there. How progressive? How safe? Where would it be wise for Brother and her to live? Mild winters, hot summers, the Boise River, a state university, a nearby military base, blacks made up about one and *a half* percent of the demographic, there'd been no known murders of blacks in recent history, it had a long-term Basque mayor, a strong art scene, was animal friendly. The state's capital, it offered more job possibilities, was only 350 miles away, seven hours by car. Doable.

For days she and Brother sat together at their computers, filled out online housing and job applications, set up interviews, scheduled city tours. She also locked down a meeting at the university.

"I hope they'll be welcoming," Brother said.

"I hope it feels like home. Either way, I'm done migrating, starting over, being a refugee in my homeland. Forty-nine moves—I'm done."

The road spills out ahead of them. Brother plays a disk by a Palestinian male singing a guttural and haunting song. He passes Prema a plastic baggy of dried fruit and mixed nuts. She takes a mango slice, hands the bag back.

"Are you planning to live with me for the rest of your life?"

"No. This is the last time."

"This is the *fifth* time. I'm your older sister, I'm not your mother."

He stares at the road. "It won't happen again."

"How won't it happen again, if you're fired for the wrong reason again, and you don't have a degree, or training, or a certificate, or money to fall back on— again?"

He says nothing.

Work had long been sketchy for Brother but got worse in the aftermath of the economic downturn. When recession-driven unemployment is high for whites, it's higher for blacks. She'd long worried about what might've happened to him had she not sent money, had he not come to live with her periodically over the years. Of course, the last time he'd had good work, before they left Texas en route to Oregon almost fifteen years ago, Brother had been generous to Prema as well. Mama had modeled love and family, generosity and devotion.

She asks, "Do you think you should finish school so you're more hirable?"

"I can't afford to go to school."

"You can't afford not to. You haven't worked for two years. You could've earned an associate degree by now."

"Please stop bringing up school. I've told you the subject is painful."

"Look," Prema says softly, "without a degree—*if* you work—you'll work twice as hard for half as much. You've got to take different actions if you want different results."

"You've been lucky."

"I've been prepared."

Silent, Brother bites the inside of his lip.

She says, "I'm going back to school cause I'm tired of being a social worker breastfeeding the whole damn world."

"You have money to go to school."

"I worked and saved money for school. You can take out a loan."

"I'm not taking out any more loans."

"Then how will you earn your own keep and pay your own way—consistently over time?"

"You just don't let up, do you?" He groans, turns

the music louder, rolls the window down, leans his shoulder and head into the surging wind.

Prema munches her fruit. She knows character strengths and character weaknesses are different sides of the same coin. Her assertiveness can be overbearing. Brother is stubborn and a dreamer. But one must be a dream-*doer*. She respects personal freedom, *and* personal responsibility. He must be able to pull his own weight. A social worker, she's acutely aware of structural inequity. She wants to help him but not enable him as he strives to find his workaround in an unjust system. She struggles to square the circle.

There are many circles to be squared. Five years ago, when Prema worked as a discharge planner in a Catholic hospital in Seattle, she was the only black employee in a department where some of the women doing the same job were paid less. She'd come under fire for speaking out in a meeting after the rich, white, male HR director stated it was *legal* for some women to be paid differently. She said *Just because it's legal doesn't make it right. Slavery was legal.*

The room froze. Trouble.

Prema led a successful unionization effort. That further stoked the ire of her superiors, whose plan was: *Cut off the head and the whole snake dies.* Before they could drum up enough excuses to fire her, she quit. She heard some of her white female co-workers got a fourteen-dollar-an-hour raise.

Blacklisted. When she walked away from her job, she walked away from her home still under water years after the financial collapse. Committed, but not attached, she'd sensed she was preparing the home for those who'd follow her. She left it in pristine condition. Still, this was a loss of legacy.

Prema's female black cat snuggled close the evening before they left Seattle. Overnight the cat died. Early next morning she took the body to the veterinarian for cremation. The ashes would be sent.

An hour before Prema's departure, a white woman neighbor of seven years knocked at her door. She said, "I'm sorry I never invited you for dinner or coffee. Are you really going to Idaho? Do you feel safe?"

"I've never felt safe."

"Please don't go there. They're not in agreement with . . . I can't imagine what it is to be a black woman in Idaho." Her eyes welled. "I'm afraid for you."

It's not just Idaho, it's America. It's not about imagining what it is to be a black woman. It's about imagining what it is to be a white woman who stands strong for equal justice.

Prema hugged her neighbor goodbye. "Please don't worry about me. I'm not going to Idaho."

Prema loaded her car with her favorite potted plants, two brindle dogs, and two male black cats. She drove behind the moving van, slushed through deep February snow across Snoqualmie Pass through eastern Washington, to Idaho, to North Idaho where she'd found work for a lot less pay in the small town of Bonners Ferry, Boundary County. Bonners Ferry was fifteen miles from the Canadian border, not far from the infamous Ruby Ridge, the site where—some years prior to her arrival—an eleven-day government standoff, shootout, and siege had taken place, and the modern American militia movement was born.

Desperate times. Desperate measures.

Among the town's two thousand five hundred people, less than one percent were members of the Kootenai Tribe. The rest were Mormons, Mennonites, and other mostly Christians, some of whom tried to convert her. In the Idaho Panhandle, remote land of rural beauty teeming with wildlife on the banks of the Kootenai River, she declined to be washed in the local blood.

It's a prepared blessing, Brother said, to encourage her and to ease his dread as she'd left him in a Seattle suburb scraping by, still seeking work. It was always hard to leave him, her only living relative. As a girl, she'd prayed for a brother. In childhood he was a Pollyanna. Where she saw a ghetto, he saw Camelot. Sometimes it seemed he'd not recovered from Mama's death, though it's been twenty years. At times he'd say, "Things would be different for me if Mama were still alive." He doesn't navigate bedrock bigotry well. Prema worries how things will be for Brother when *she* dies.

He'd followed her from Texas to Oregon where, repeatedly, he'd been wrongfully fired. At the time they lived there, Oregon was home to the highest number of KKK outside the South. In Wood Village, outside Portland, her next-door neighbor's son flew the Confederate flag from the antenna of his truck, displayed crossed rifles in his rear window, walked his pit bull on a chain.

At least for a while Brother had a supportive partner. She'd hoped against hope things would work out well.

On Prema's first day in Bonners Ferry, she saw a new red car afloat in the Kootenai River, headlights on, *Proud to Be an American Democrat* bumper sticker still attached. A big white pickup pulled away from the bank. Emblazoned in its rear window: *Don't Californicate Idaho.* Prema's prayer: *God, just don't let me die in Bonners Ferry.*

On her first night at the rented blue house in the woods, her younger male black cat clawed at the front door, yowling to go outside. He was never seen again. Co-workers surmised *Owl probably got him. Or a coyote. They eat small dogs and cats.* Fortunately, her two dogs were large, and her other black cat, shrewd.

As the lone social worker at the local hospital and nursing home—where the oldest resident was 105—she coordinated patient discharges and resident admissions; assessed and monitored their mental health; arranged specialty appointments; and secured transportation for major surgeries, hemorrhoid and ingrown toenail removals, colonoscopies, eyeglasses, hearing aids, and false teeth. She provided big-dog therapy visits, coordinated pie-and-ice cream socials, raised money for special events, attended to their psychosocial needs. She paused when she overheard one elder say: *Stay humble, you never know what you come to fore you die.*

By spring she heaved bags of black oil sunflower seeds from the feed store to the blue house and filled twenty-five bird feeders each week. *We useta have birds at our place before you came here* one neighbor said. Prema stacked salt-lick cubes and deer blocks on the covered front porch, then dragged them to the side yard for deer that stood waiting near her car for breakfast, deer that lingered with their babies in the driveway at day's end as if with their hands on their hips asking, *Where's our dinner?* Mama deer that, during hunting season, one lazy neighbor just opened his windows, shot, and hauled away.

Prema had a backyard fence built around aromatic Poet's Wife roses; she planted Honeycrisp and Zestar apple trees, Queen Anne and Rainier cherry trees for those who'd come after her. Beyond the fence—maybe too close to the house—she planted a Mcintosh tree so the bears and deer would have good apples after she'd come and gone.

During her first months in Bonners Ferry she was repeatedly stopped by police. A hospital administrator suggested Prema write an article about herself and her position and put it, with her picture, in the newspaper to introduce herself to law enforcement and to the town. One hospital cook said: *In a small town everybody's in everybody's business. They're all especially gonna wanna know your story. You hafta tell em somethin. To keep your ducks in a row and your turds in a herd, decide what you want em to know, then tell em that, otherwise they'll make up somethin and spread it all over town like jam. And remember—don't ever say nothin bad bout nobody—cause you're probably talkin to their cousin.*

The newspaper published Prema's story. The police stops abated.

Snow flurries ended in March and resumed in September. Every six months was a winter whiteout prayer. Her mantra, as she drove five miles an hour in her five-mile winter radius: *God, please don't let me slide off this mountain road.* Another, when she'd pull into a wrong driveway in the blind blur of white powder three feet deep: *God, please, don't let them shoot me.*

Silver icicles hung thick from the eaves to the ground. Snow piled midway up the windows, draped Douglas fir, cloaked Ponderosa pine. She hardcore shoveled snow for the first time. Before she knew to buy Les Schwab's *big ugly siped studded snow tires* she'd slid, skidded, spun, and barreled into multiple berms— a new word in her vocabulary—and thanked neighbor men who pulled her car from frozen ditches.

Better buck up black woman she told herself. And buck up she did.

Like most folks, she ate her way through winters, gained five pounds a year, laughed when locals called it, "The Bonners Ferry spread." She was baptized into backwoods life by one neighbor who knocked, gifted her warm zucchini bread, came in, looked around, found her Japanese raku pottery and African batiks strange. The neighbor'd expected to see mounted heads.

Another neighbor rolled out the rural red carpet, helped her cut her country teeth on hunks of bear link, yak burger, and deer-elk sausage all in one day. Alone, except for her companion animals, she journaled long in the loud silence of winter nights, blessed the soul of her son, Mahal, who'd died so young.

Within six months she could distinguish rabbit poop from deer poop from elk poop on the side yard, behind the house, and in the back woods. She watched wild turkeys, deer, and elk—or maybe they were moose and caribou—roam the back roads. She heard armageddonists, survivalists, and outlaws stock-piled food and guns in the mountains; was told that religious men who lived just across the border had multiple wives in town and traveled back and forth for conjugal visits, while the sister-wives collected welfare stateside. She didn't smoke, drink, or use drugs, but she learned that Canadian bud flowed freely through the town. When a man known to make meth in a house down the road walked dazed through her back yard, she felt threatened enough to call police.

To show her good will, Prema distributed six months of small gifts—exotic chocolate bars, designer caramel corn, and orchids—to random people: her landlord and lady, property managers, strangers, co-workers, patients, residents, mailmen, people at the post office, folks at the dump, and especially to the lady who always wore pink, pursed her lips, smiled, and said *Just cause I work at the dump don't mean I can't be pretty.* Prema delivered gifts to her new dentist's office where a sign read: *You only have to brush the ones you want to keep.*

Brother rubs his calves and asks, "Can we stop and stretch our legs?"

Prema looks out the window at the vast expanse of wilderness. "Not yet."

"Why not? I'm getting a cramp."

"Deal with it, Brother. We'll stop at a place where there are other people around."

It's been a while since Brother's former partner was around. A few years ago, he was heartbroken after his sweet Filipino boyfriend left him for another man. Brother'd visited Prema for two weeks during that scorched Bonners Ferry summer, the year lightning sparked fire in the mountains, fire that jumped the river, drove wildlife into town, smoked the air, bloodied the sun, left the taste of char in his mouth, pained and painted the whites of his eyes red. A mountain lion stalked in Prema's front yard, a black bear rummaged through trash cans, a coyote skulked around the backyard pond. *Whoa. Frontierswoman. Sister's got lady balls.*

When the smoke cleared, to help cheer him up, Prema drove Brother past silos, cows, earless goats, alpaca farms, to the river, to the teeny farmer's market in the tiny downtown, introduced him to the wildlife refuge, to huckleberries and wild morels, treated him to breakfast at the Badger's Den, lunch at Mugsy's, dinner at the Rusty Moose. That June she'd already started "winterizing." A productive worrier, she was always planning ahead, preparing, stocking up as a defense against the bottom ever falling out. Being together lifted their spirits. She sent him home with a care package of local treats. He'd been grateful to visit, but rural life was not his feng shui. To him, life in North Idaho was a descent into hell—a special suite.

Prema'd told him of her experiences with two coworkers. One had given her a backhanded compliment by saying she was a *snake killer*—someone who's relentless, who doesn't back off, who'll keep hitting a snake until she kills it.

The other co-worker, a red-haired nurse had, out of nowhere, gotten in Prema's face in front of a supervisor, patients, God, and country and said, "Fuck you, bitch."

When the supervisor did nothing, Prema took her lunch break, loaded up the dogs, drove to the river, and handwrote a scalding letter detailing the incident, calling for appropriate disciplining of the nurse. She drove back to her office, typed the letter, emailed it to the CEO and HR Director, and copied the manager, supervisor, offending co-worker, and herself. Before sending it, she added a PS:

"Get it right. Not bitch. Black *dragon* bitch."

Trouble.

It was hard for Brother to get a job. Prema always got work but had to fight to keep it, get fair pay, get respect. She leans into rather than away from trouble.

Prema checks the mirrors and the gas gauge. "Hey, did I tell you about my conversation with that Mennonite man at the gas station in Bonners Ferry?"

Brother shakes his head.

"When I went inside to pay, he asked me, How're you gettin along? How's folks been treatin you here? I told him I was OK. He said it wasn't long ago 'colored' people couldn't spend the night in Boundary County, they could pass through but fore sunset, they had to get on up to Canada or get on back to Sandpoint. 'Coloreds' couldn't stay the night, much less live in Bonners Ferry. Then he asked: How long you plannin on stayin?"

Brother mulls this over. "Bass-ackwards. Fifty years behind the times. Things'll be better in Boise."

"Boise's Idaho. Idaho's America, our motherland —built on stolen land, enslavement, and genocide. We'll hope for the best, prepare for the worst, confront what comes, work like hell."

He sips coffee from his Thermos.

Prema says, "I know Mama'd expect me to secure a safe place for us."

"You don't think I can make it on my own, do you?"

"I don't think you ever have a plan B."

He stares out the window.

Desperate to leave Bonners Ferry after three years, determined to get close enough to Moscow to attend the University of Idaho, Prema accepted a therapist position in St. Maries, another North Idaho town of 2,600 people near the St. Joe, St. Maries, and Coeur d'Alene Rivers, not far from the Coeur d'Alene Reservation, an hour from Hayden Lake, original home of the Aryan Nations.

Prior to relocating, Prema visited the nearby town of Plummer, where, when she walked into the Warpath Trading Post, a male tribal member said *I want you to meet the only white woman in St. Maries who married a black man.* He introduced her to the German widow of Vernon Joseph Baker, a WWII veteran who, fifty-two years *after* the war, was awarded the Medal of Honor for his valor. Mrs. Baker gasped with surprise and happiness to see an American of African ancestry. She confided in Prema that some in St. Maries hadn't treated her husband well.

Prema rented one of the few available houses close to town—a hundred-year-old, four-thousand-square-foot purple Victorian mansion that she dubbed The Old Purple Queen on the Hill. Grand yet misplaced, its three stories towered over trailer homes in the valley. At the back of the east driveway loomed a spaceship-sized propane tank. October leaves from a pair of century-old oaks embellished the front yard, amassing in auric mounds on the ground, on the graveled north driveway, on the dirt road. Tree roots crawled beneath the house, bulged, cracked through the basement's concrete foundation, and choked the drain, which required repeated augering for sake of the septic tank. Rumor had it the house was haunted. Not haunted. Colored. Purple. Gossip was Prema's big dogs were vicious. Not vicious. Large. Dark.

Above the town on a much higher hill, in view of the Purple Queen, a formidable wooden cross stood guard over the valley. It shone bright with Christmas lights every night of the year. In the Catholic strong-hold of Benewah County, there was rivalry between Native Americans on the county's west side and white folks on the east side. Amid closed silver mines, dwindling sawmills, and hidden meth labs, there was bad blood over water rights. There were whispers of Christian Identity groups, anti-government patriots.

God, deliver me from St. Maries.

Prema's new post included duties as the sole state Designated Examiner appointed to assess patients' needs for involuntary psychiatric hospitalization in a county of nine thousand people. As it was deemed unwise for her to enter people's houses and trailers, those in mental health crisis were referred to her at the office or at the ER across the street. Early on, after being stopped twice by police, her boss advised *Tell em you're here helping the Sheriff. And mention me—everybody knows Johnny.* That helped.

Prema yawns, rubs her eyes, rolls down the window, breathes. "Talk to me so I don't get sleepy."

Brother watches scenery whooshing by. "It's hard to believe I've lived in Idaho for a year."

"Believe it."

"It's sad not to have gotten even a minimum wage job."

"It's *sadder* that the minimum wage is $7.25 an hour."

"Who can live on that?"

"People who inherited generational wealth. Not us." They laugh.

"I'm so glad we're moving." Brother claps his hands. "I won't ever get work in North Idaho."

"But, until we move, you should keep trying."

Soon after Prema moved to St. Maries, the demands of her workload wiped school off the table.

A year later, Brother asked if he and his cat could move in with her. Desperate times, desperate measures.

That night she had a dream and awakened screaming. The next day her black cat, following as she walked the dogs, was struck by a car. He howled for her from the core of his being. She turned, saw him paralyzed, drove him to the vet, sobbing.

Each death signaled change.

To help prepare Brother for life on the ground in St. Maries, Prema shared with him how the big dogs had awakened her on New Year's Eve, shivering. It was 45 degrees *inside* the Purple Queen. The propane tank, that cost nine hundred a month to fill in winter, was empty. They must be frugal. Also, the mail lady'd warned her it wouldn't be a safe walk on certain roads, near certain trailer homes, not even with the two big dogs. They must be vigilant. And, two of her adult neighbors—not the kind neighbors in the trailer across the north driveway, not sweet Miss Lu down the road, but the ones across the east driveway, the ones with swastika inkwork —had refused to speak to her for the better part of a year. Still, their five-year-old daughter kindled a conversation.

Are you a black person?

Yes.

Are you sure you're a black person?

I'm sure.

My daddy calls black people . . .

It takes a lot of love. It takes more than love.

One afternoon at the post office, a pregnant black woman ran down the stairs as Prema climbed up. They passed each other, did a doubletake, then the woman rushed back and embraced Prema while her older white husband waited in the car with their three young children. *"Sister, where are you from?"* Prema asked.

"Florida. How about you?"

"Texas. How long've you been here?"

"Four years. You?"

"In St. Maries, two."

She grasped Prema's hands. *"But I've never seen you before."*

Her name was Sunny. At an abject point she'd met her husband online. He had a job, a house on fifteen acres with a crick. He sent a ticket. Desperate times, desperate measures. She gave up oranges for chokecherries, had a child each year, a fourth on the way. Noticing her husband's side-eye, they hurriedly exchanged numbers. Sunny never called. Never answered Prema's calls.

Brother, if you want to see a black person here, besides me, you'd better look in the mirror.

High sun beams slightly east of due south. They've been on the road for several hours. Brother points to a public rest stop on the lip of the Salmon River where people sit in several parked cars. It looks like a good place to stretch their legs and walk the dogs.

Brother gets out, squats, stretches, smooths his dark creased jeans, re-tucks his starched white shirt, then stands marveling at a scene he'd love to sketch: sequestered within the steep canyon walls, a sparse cluster of attractive homes face the Seven Devils Mountains. Large, open windows overlook the comings and goings of the valley, the river, the rest stop.

Brother watches his sister position the dog ramp at the hatch door, then lead the leashed dogs down. Her Mexican silver bracelets jangle as she grabs a handful of plastic poop-patrol bags from the back seat. She has strong features. In her long black linen tunic, matching palazzo pants, African headscarf, and violet-blue lipstick, she's a striking portrait against the lavender day and pink sky. He appreciates that his sister is one of a few who can pull off wearing bohemian clothing in places where the fashion statement is camouflage and on-trend adornments are ammo and guns.

Prema hands Brother some bags for safekeeping, then shuts the hatch, leaving the ramp extended. She smiles at people in cars near them on either side. Some smile back, wave, call out greetings and admiration for the sibling dogs—Corazon, the hundred-pound female, and Amour, the hundred-and-fifty-pound male.

They walk the pebbled path along the length of the

rest stop, skirting the edge of clear water that snakes across black rocks jutting beside and below them. The dogs' brindle coats gleam with golden stripes in warm sunlight. They saunter, wag their tails, sniff, and pee. Air near the river is cool, scented with late spring.

They chat about Boise; his dream to land a good job, have health insurance, his own place, a studio, another partner; her hopes to send down roots and train to become a writer. They make a lazy loop back to the car. Prema leads the happy dogs up the ramp and into the hatch, gives each a bowl of water, a treat, a hug, then shuts the door.

Beside the car, Brother pivots in a slow circle, again taking in the panorama of isolated woods, the mountains beyond, and the nearby houses sheathed in the hollow hillside. From wide-mouthed windows the whitest curtains billow above the canyon toward the peak called Devils Throne.

He stops, looks at Prema. "I feel like someone's watching us."

A car at the rest stop pulls off.

"Come on, Brother, let's go."

As Prema collapses the ramp, a law enforcement vehicle screeches into the rest stop and parks behind her. The officer leans forward, peers at her license plate, calls in the number.

She and Brother look at each other wide-eyed.

Prema whispers, "Did these white people call the cops on us?"

The uniformed officer exits the patrol car. Forties, tall, white, armed. He walks toward Prema. Travelers in the other vehicles stare, then speed away.

Prema surveys the scene. *No witnesses.* Her heart pounds. She recalls having once seen a white male policeman stand, with billy club in hand, above a young black man lying on the ground, hog tied—chest down, wrists and ankles bound together high behind his arched back—his dark eyes pleading.

"Officer, did we do something wrong?" she asks, "Are leashed dogs not allowed to be walked here? We didn't see a sign."

"They didn't poop," Brother says. "We have bags." He shows a handful. "We always pick up if they do." He rubs sweat from his palm against his jeans.

The officer looks Brother up and down, spots his tiny gold hoop earring, smirks. "Just checkin on you— bein sure everything's all right here. Wanted to see if you're OK."

He stopped to check on us, but not on others who'd been parked here? God.

She remembers the story of Joe Campos Torres, a young Vietnam War veteran, arrested, repeatedly beaten by police officers, never taken to jail, his body found washed up on the banks of Buffalo Bayou.

"Sir, why did you call in my license plate number?"

He ignores her question, looks at the ramp. "I notice you have dogs. What kind are they?"

Please, let this go well. "Bullmastiffs."

"I work with dogs."

Brother's voice quivers. "Would you like to meet ours?"

The officer nods.

Prema side glances at Brother. *Be quiet.* She leans the ramp against the car and opens the hatch.

Cautious, the officer looks in. The handsome six-year-old littermates sit, friendly, docile, panting in midday heat. He scans the car, eyes the cat carrier on the back seat.

"Where are you coming from?"

What? That's not your business. "Northern Idaho," she says.

"From St. Maries," says Brother.

"Where are you going?"

Why is he questioning us? "Southern Idaho," Prema answers.

Brother adds, "To Boise." Under his armpits are huge wet rings.

"What will you do there?"

"Sightsee," Prema says.

"Look for a place to move," says Brother.

"Where are you staying?"

"La Quinta Inn," she says.

Brother locks his knees to curb the shaking. "They accept animals."

Prema's mind flashes to the batons of multiple white policemen beating Rodney King, striking him more than fifty times on a shushed California evening, the headlights of passing cars washing shadows over his floundering body.

The officer gets a call on the radio near his left shoulder. He tries to muffle the sound with his right hand. The voice on the other end says, "It checked out OK."

Brother takes an audible breath.

The officer's eyes dart to Prema's headwrap, to the Asian letter and small black snake tattooed on her right forearm, to her nails, like her lips, meticulously painted indigo.

"Are you a Muslim?"

Oh God. "No."

He looks at Brother. "I train dogs," he nods toward his vehicle. "Mine is in the car."

Brother asks, "What kind is it?"

She tasers him with her eyes. *Fool.*

"German Shepherd."

Brother swallows hard, smiles. "Can we meet him? We love German Shepherds—don't we, Prema? We used to have two when we were little. Mama named them Schatzelein and Blitzkrieg. And they—"

"Brother!" Her tone silences him. She looks at the officer, searches the slate blue eyes in his almost handsome face, takes note as he inventories the diamond in her nostril, her handcrafted eagle-feather silver earrings, her three old pawn Navajo turquoise rings. She equals him in height. His cowboy hat is weathered, his brown boots scuffed, on each foot bunions protrude, his belt and holster are worn. On his left hand, the tip of his middle finger is missing, he wears a tungsten wedding band.

She recollects two white policemen standing near a city entrance sign:

DON'T LET THE SUN GO DOWN
ON YOU IN VIDOR

She gauges his body language. *Slave patroller.* "What's

your dog trained to do?" She listens for intent behind his words.

"Search for drugs."

"What kind of drugs?"

"Marijuana, cocaine, heroin, meth."

She slows her breathing, wills herself to remain calm.

"I see." *I hope you didn't plant anything in my car.* "We don't have any of those."

"Then it's OK for me to let her out."

That wasn't a question. "Yes."

She remembers images, hears babel—white policemen aiming high-powered hoses on unarmed black children, police siccing attack dogs on peaceful black protestors for equal justice, for human rights.

Sun burns cold. Time suspends. There is no wind. River is hushed. Prema stands, narrowed eyes vigilant. She is still.

The officer opens the patrol car door, releases his dog—a young wiry gray female; she darts to the SUV, sniffs, circles it, sniffs carefully, sniffs intently, sniffs repeatedly.

Brother crosses himself. The officer observes the dog. Prema watches the officer, his hand on his gun. *God help us.*

Involuntarily, Brother shudders.

The police dog sits at attention near the rear tire of the SUV. She waits, having found nothing. The officer removes his hand from his holster and signals. The dog relaxes. The officer hocks, spits on the ground.

Giddy with relief, Brother says, "Oh, she's

beautiful." He fans himself with the empty plastic poop bags. "Can we give her a treat?"

The officer nods.

Prema glares at Brother, her teeth clenched. She retrieves the bag of dog treats from the car, steps forward, shows the officer ingredients listed on the package. He's uninterested. She hands him a treat, he gives it to his dog, the dog gobbles it down. Again, he signals. The dog leaps into the rear of the patrol car. He shuts the door and stands, ill at ease.

Prema closes the bag of treats, tosses it into her car, squints at the officer's badge.

"Kozlowski. Officer Kozlowski, you're of Polish ancestry."

His eyebrows raise. "How'd you know that?"

I can read. "I went to a Polish elementary school."

"Where?"

"Ohio. Helen Sowinski. I've eaten lots of cabbage rolls and pierogi."

He quarter-smiles, looks at her car. "I see your license plate honors Peace Officers."

"After graduate school, I helped train Texas officers on abuse of power, oppression, and domination. I worked with Crisis Intervention Team Officers who were learning to talk down mentally ill patients rather than shoot them down. Have you heard of that training?"

He shakes his head.

"During intake at a psychiatric emergency center, I helped officers filling out paperwork spell *schizophrenia*."

He half-smiles.

"I provided emotional support to rookies who'd seen their first suicide. In Oregon I was a therapist and an HIV and Hep C counselor at an all-male prison."

"Which one?"

"Columbia River. Word was that some guards had been sexual with offenders."

"And now?

"I've completed my work in Benewah County. I treated mental health patients at a clinic. I assessed patients in crisis for the hospital and for the sheriff. Locals say a prisoner dug himself out of the jail with a plastic spoon."

He stifles a chuckle. "I heard about that."

"Do you have a family, Officer?"

"Yep." He beams. "Four kids. My two sons and I do a lot of sportin, huntin, and fishin.

"And you?"

"My child died. He'd be twenty-three had he lived."

He looks at the ground. "Sorry, ma'am."

"Your wife must worry about you being out here."

"She does."

"I wish you safety."

"Appreciate it. I plan to retire in ten years. Course, if you want to hear God laugh, tell Him your plans, right?"

Brother nods.

"Sounds like a good plan," Prema says. "It's time for us to get back on the road."

Brother adds, "So we can arrive in daylight."

Prema sees the sun has moved further west. "How far is the next gas station?"

He points, "Thirty miles south as the crow flies."

She makes eye contact, steps toward him, extends her right hand.

He again notices her tattoos. "What's the snake mean?"

"It means snake."

"And the word?"

"My name in Sanskrit. Prema. It means love."

He's quizzical. "You love snakes?"

"God loves snakes. It reminds me of my goal to love as God loves, without compromise."

She reaches out again. They shake hands in parting. His hand, smaller than hers, seems fragile. "Much love to you and to your family."

He opens the patrol car door, tips his hat. "Yes, ma'am. Good talkin to you."

She raises her hand. "Please wait, Officer Kozlowski. One thing more."

He pauses, steps forward, looks at her.

"What caused you to stop and call in my license plate number?"

He doesn't respond.

"Black people are much more likely, than others, to be stopped by police. And we're far less likely, than others, to fare well in those encounters."

He's quiet.

"It would help you to know why you stopped us, so it doesn't happen again."

He wipes his nose with the back of his hand, gives no answer.

"What if your minister asked? What if someone stopped your wife?"

He lowers his head. "Protocol. Just protocol, ma'am." He retreats to his car and drives away.

As the patrol car disappears in a trail of dust, Prema wonders what, if anything, the officer might be thinking.

She and Brother look at each other. Silent, they climb into the SUV. She locks the doors, and after the click, she sighs.

Brother fastens his seat belt. "That was *really* weird. Surreal." He puts his fingers inside the carrier, touches the cat. "We're safe now, Kitty."

"He had no reason to detain us. And you were so nervous you couldn't stop talking. Brother, if we're ever stopped again—unless you're *asked* something— please be quiet. Especially for you, this could have gone another way."

"Yeah." He's thoughtful. "I was just trying to be a social butterfly, like Mama, so he'd know we weren't suspicious. He was a nice guy, kind of."

"A nice guy, a biased mind, a loaded gun."

Somber, he looks out at river waves slow-dancing in blue. "Thankfully, this time, things turned out OK."

Thankfully.

Prema memorizes this incident. She memorizes the rest stop on the Nez Perce ancestral lands near Seven Devils Mountains not far from Hells Canyon, the canyon carved by the Snake River, into which the Salmon River of No Return flows.

She starts the engine, drives south in silence alongside the rising and falling water—from White

Bird through Lucille and into Riggins where people at the gas station are kind; where the river divides the state, and the time zone shifts from Pacific to Mountain; where northern Idaho ends and southern Idaho begins. She drives on. The dogs rest. Brother dozes, his head against the windowpane, his face innocent, troubled, worn. She'd prayed for a brother and helped raise him. Brother is an answered prayer. She must prepare a safe place for him. Plant roses in Mama's name, irises for the black cats, lilies in memory of her son, Mahal.

Under an achromatic sky, in towns between Riggins and McCall, she drives past waving Confederate flags. Soon geography will transition from forest to high desert. The tires whish along the road. She pushes away images of crosses burning in Charlottesville, the churn and drone of alt-right words, "You will not replace us. Jews will not replace us," signs of rising white separatism, white national-ism, white supremacism.

Prema presses forward. Will Boise be different? Perhaps. Will she be different? She vows to be herself no matter where it leads her, to meet life as it is and cre-ate from there. She inserts a CD, turns the volume low. A Sahrawi woman sings in Arabic, a song of protest, mourning, beauty. Prema looks at her name and at the black snake tattooed on her forearm. Love. Protectress. Regeneration. Creative life force. One hundred more miles. May all be well.

➤

Like None Other
Jamie Figueroa

THREE DAYS AFTER WE MOVED IN, WE WOKE TO rabbits in the yard. Instead of lean and large-footed creatures, flecked with desert camouflage, black eyes tight and suspicious, ears vertical as if starched and pinned to the tops of their heads—they were, well, black and white and impossible, plump with long, shiny hair, and red-eyed, as if from an illustration in a children's book. A whole herd of them.

"A sign," said my daughter, Micah, mini carrots crammed in each fist. She knelt on a box of books. Books I might not live long enough to unpack. Her long legs evidence of a growth spurt at fifteen. "Eleven," she chanted, as if she were about to launch into a nursery rhyme. "Eleven."

"Surely someone will come for them," I said in her direction. She'd told me the previous night I wasn't allowed to look at her anymore. She'd told me that my staring was an oppressive force, a threat to her independence. "Can't you see I'm not an extension of your body?" she'd said. "If you want to stare at someone, stare at yourself." What she did not say was, "Can't you see I'm not an extension of your sick body?"

We'd been unpacking the kitchen, and I had too many plates in my arms. Trying to lift them into the cupboard made me shake, my weakness exposed. The overhead fixture was missing two out of its three light bulbs. We squinted into haphazardly marked boxes, trying to make sense of what the wads of packing paper contained. All around us, paper covered the floor.

"Am I supposed to answer that?" I'd said. "Isn't it obvious?" I'd stopped pretending I knew how to respond to her months before I made the decision to move us five states west and a block away from her father, his second wife, their three children, their relatives, and all their relatives' relatives.

"Are you asking for my permission?" Micah's strength was undiluted. I admired it. I told myself it would keep her from getting sick. I told myself it was better for her to be angry with me than grief-stricken. Anger was combustible. Fuel for living.

"Lost," I said into the dust coating the screen door. I kept my focus on the rabbits, careful not to ignite Micah. "Every one of you. Lost."

Huddled among scrub grass, goat's heads, dandelions, and mounds of pebbles, their velvet coats shone in the early morning sun. Each coat a different combination of black on white, or white on black. Floppy ears folded along their sides, twitching noses tilted downward. Clearly, they were the kind that should've been kept in outdoor pens constructed for the purpose, or else in the garage. Or inside the house all together, sheltered. I was reminded of fat cats, or cows grazing. I was reminded of what rabbits should look like. I thought, These are tame, ornamental cousins. Decorative homogeny. I wished for the days when I still believed in my ability to write poetry. I felt empty and, suddenly, missed being pretty more than I had let myself until then. I still had hair, the jagged tips of which frayed around my shoulders. To conceal the thinning patches on my scalp, I had tied a scarf around my head. The first time Micah saw me this way, she'd accused me of appropriation.

"Didn't everyone's ancestors have material they tied to their heads?" I'd said. "Especially the women?"

"Are you speaking from your particular ancestry or from your blanket whiteness?" Micah said. The daughter I raised to be well-read, articulate, aware. My daughter. As dark as her father, her features an echo of his. No evidence of me at all.

"A sign," Micah said, again, of the rabbits. "Magic welcomes us." Her sword had turned into a wand; instead of a warrior, she was a little girl again. She slipped around me and out the door. The rabbits lifted their heads, throbbing noses and bouquets of whiskers pointed in Micah's direction. They did not seem to know enough to run from her. Instead they crept in closer, creating a crude semi-circle, as if she were going to tell them a story.

Sunlight illuminated the back of her. For early June it seemed persistent and invasive but this was the high desert, and we were at 7,000 feet. The hottest month, we were warned, until the rains came. If the rains came. I watched the eloquent curve of her long neck stretch forward. As she bent down and kneeled, the soles of her bare feet peeled away from the ground. Gym shorts folded over at her waist, tank top exposing midriff. All of her wet, dark hair secured to the top of her head. The expanse of her endless, healthy limbs exposed.

I used to smell her. Before she could walk, and for years after, I'd plant my nose in her hair and in the crook of her neck. Just days ago it seemed, I used to hold her feet in my hands as if they were bars of gold. "You are made of gold," I'd say. How long would she hear my voice saying this? I didn't hear my mother or my grandmother, not anymore. But every time I looked in the mirror, I saw them, an image of comfort and of death. Ours was a family inheritance the women carried. Each daughter waiting her turn.

"Don't get bit." I heard his voice before I could see him. Rounding the broken fence of our front yard, a young man, shorter than Micah. He was laughing at his own joke while she looked him up and down. Flip flops and a woven grass hat tied under his chin, white tracks of sunscreen marking his hairless jawline. "They found you."

"Are they yours?" Micah said.

"No," he said, "they're yours."

She turned toward the house. Looked at the screen door I was leaning against. It wasn't protection she was after; it was simply closeness, though I knew she'd reject me if I got near.

"What? You don't want them?" It was obvious he wanted to make her smile, but she refused to give him that gift. She'd make him work for it, like she did anyone who wasn't her father.

"Do they really bite?" Her fists rose to her hips.

He must have had an idea of what her stance meant because he held out his hand, as if surrendering.

"Miguel," he said. "de la Torre."

"I know what that means," she said. "Bull."

"Is it that obvious?"

One side of her mouth began to creep its way up. "Where'd they come from?" she said, barely shaking his hand before letting it go.

"And you are?"

"Living here now." She widened her stance. "The rabbits?"

"They're Pierre's rabbits. Or they were. He's gone now. Back to France—immigration or something—I don't know, but his girlfriend did this."

"Did what?" Micah said.

"Freed them." He fiddled with the string under his chin. In spite of the heat, he'd left the sleeves of his blue linen shirt unrolled. The small buttons at his wrists were not fastened. Once a dress shirt, now a work shirt, I guessed. His pants, stained with dirt, were thinning at the knees. "He ate them."

"What?" She pulled her fists into her armpits, her arms a tight cross.

"Pierre. He ate them. Like chickens," he said, forcing a laugh. "After he killed them, of course."

Micah's face creased in horror. "What do you mean?"

The rabbits chewed the carrots close to her feet.

"It's a French thing. He'd invite us over, me and my uncle, and the Garcias and the Trujillos and the Apodacas." He pointed at various houses down the street. "And even those Canadians that came a few years back." He paused, studying Micah's face. "They tasted good."

When I was young, we ate squirrel and rabbit. My mother gathered what she didn't grow, shot what she didn't harvest. She came from a long line of women from the woods. First Germany and then the Midwest. Women who could peel the hide from a four-legged animal, stew the meat, boil the bones. When I was a child, it was not uncommon for me to have to walk around a doe strung from the elm tree in the front yard. Blood draining, soaking into the ground. She'd give me the rabbit's fluff of tail to rub between my fingers, until eventually it would come undone, hair covering my palms.

Once she was diagnosed, she stopped hunting. She died within the year. I never told Micah any of this. Never took her into the woods, never showed her how to distinguish tracks. Instead, I taught her to question, to critique. The weapons I'd learned in college, where I was the first to go. That's where I met her father. I let him tell her who she was, and I held her feet, told her she was gold.

The rabbits hopped across the driveway, negotiated the sidewalk, crossed the street. While they didn't form a line, they did seem to move somewhat together. After a few minutes, I saw them under the parked cars in the neighbor's driveway.

"Cream sauce," the young man said, "lots of cream sauce." He pushed up the brim of his hat. "But I'm not going to kill them. I am going to trap them though, tonight. Could use your yard for one or two of the traps."

Micah shook her head.

"Come on," he said. More laughter—decoration, it seemed, for his words. "I can't do it without your permission."

I stepped forward then, the screen door banging behind me. "Yes, please." I hugged the shade of the stucco; the medication made my skin burn instantly in the sun. "They're not safe roaming like this. Use as many traps as you need to."

Micah tore out of the yard and disappeared from sight. In an hour, I'd need to call and have her father send her back. There was work to do. This would be her house after I was gone.

The sound of the swamp cooler gurgled down the hall. All the shades were pulled except on the north side, where I had a perfectly good view of the garage and trash bins next door. The mesas and cottonwoods were only to be imagined from here. Still, it was better than no view at all. Occasionally, a crow would land on the bins and peer into the gravel below, turn its head my way.

I tried to stay awake. I wanted to stay awake for as many hours of the day as I possibly could. But I felt like I was moving through wet sand. My head felt double its size and weight. My eyelids were heavy. It took us a week to make the drive, three hours on the road a day, a slow crawl lasting nearly 1,300 miles. "We're paying tribute to the wagon migration," I'd told Micah, trying to be the fun mother with cancer, instead of just the mother with cancer.

"The ones with or without slaves?" she returned without hesitation. "Or the ones that killed Indians and then took their land?" She'd wanted to learn how to drive on the way, but the car was overpacked. It was hard to see, and then there were the storms. One after another until we reached west Texas. West. Texas. Which made me think more about Hell than any dying woman ever should.

I didn't hear them knocking—Micah and her father, Siler. They surprised me at the window, scaring off the crow, and disrupting my view of the trash bins.

"What did I tell you?" Micah said, looking up at him. Her voice was muffled, but I had no trouble hearing it. "We've been knocking," she said, then cupped her hands and pressed them to the glass. I could see her eyelashes from the couch.

"Helen," Siler shouted. "Door's locked." He winked at me, grinning.

This was Siler's permanent expression since we'd arrived a few days ago. A constant smile without showing his teeth. The punctuation of winks. He'd met the moving truck before our arrival and helped unpack it and the furniture had been arranged in configurations I'd never have chosen. The beds too close to the closets. The dining room table jutting into the kitchen, instead of up against the wall. The couch facing the window where we could study the trash bins next door and birds that seemed too heavy to fly. From some point outside of myself, I watched myself confused by it. I watched myself not saying anything. I watched myself watching, mostly.

"We'll have keys cut tomorrow," Siler said, as he and Micah walked past me into the house. "There's a shop down the street." He stopped and lifted his chin, drawing in a long breath. "It doesn't smell right in here."

"It's her," Micah said. She was already at the freezer, pulling out a bag of cherries.

"You didn't just say that about your mother."

She smiled, her whole face reconfiguring with joy. "Dad. Daaaaaad."

"Micah." His voice dropped. Still, he was gentle with her. "Don't make me tell you what you already know."

"I'm joking," she said, squirming on her tiptoes like she did when she was six. "I'm sorry, Helen. Cherries?"

She'd started calling me Helen when my remission

ended. We had many sessions of counseling. If using my name made her feel more in control and she could begin to negotiate a distance that would only grow, then fine. Helen.

"Are you going to feed me with your hands?" I said to her. "Or do you remember where the utensils are?"

"Gross," she said. "No one's eating with their hands."

"Do you know where anything is?" I said to Siler. "I can't find half of the boxes."

Grin. Wink. "In the shed out back."

"Because it's easy for me to haul them in?"

"Because you'll be able to move around easier in here and not hurt yourself."

The logic of the Ex never changes. Five years of marriage. One daughter. I kept the house and the life. He reinvented himself in a place where people drive to see the stars at night, hear coyote choruses, and eat chile poured over every meal. "Red or green, Helen," Micah kept asking as we drove closer.

"Probably, neither, Micah," I answered, which only made her ask again. Insistent. She needed me to commit, to promise.

I wouldn't comment on the placement of the furniture.

"Thanks, Dad," Micah said, "for not dumping all the boxes in here." She produced two spoons, rinsed them, and placed a cherry in one. As she handed it to me, she whispered, "I didn't mean it." She made sure my grip was secure before removing her hand.

"Rabbits?" Siler said.

"Eleven," Micah said, her eyes wide. She wiggled her nose. Stuck out her tongue, which was already t urning red from the cherries. "The cutest, cutest, cutest."

The way a daughter came to life with her father.

"Tricksters."

"What?" I said.

"The rabbits. Like coyote. Watch out." He leaned back against the counter, resting his foot against the bottom rung of a barstool. "Did you talk to them?"

He'd grown out his hair. It draped over his chest in tightly coiled dreads. He had one long feather tattooed on each of his forearms. He smelled like coconut oil. A small leather pouch hung from his neck, some sort of talisman I guessed. When he saw me staring at it, he tucked it under his T-shirt, which read, WATER IS LIFE, in bold blue script.

"Talk to them?" I said. "And say what?"

"Got to ask yourself, Helen. Why you woke up on the day of the new moon, three days after arriving, with a yard bursting at the seams with tricksters."

"It's the new moon?" Micah said.

"What happens on the new moon?" I said.

"Plant your intentions," Siler said. Grin. Wink.

"Plant them where?" I said.

"Where?" He burst into laughter.

"Mom," Micah said. "What are your intentions?"

She'd slipped and hadn't even noticed. Mom. She was bright, all teeth, her smile exploding. Siler stood behind her, shaking his head. He'd heard it too.

Long after my mother died, the memory of bathing her remained. I had been awkward, unable to recall the way she'd done it with her mother, even though I was there at her side watching. I was too young to hold the details. She'd had help—my grandmother's sisters. I didn't want to be alone with my mother's body at the end. When the nurse asked if I wanted to take her home, I said nothing. After her last breath, life was still happening up and down the hall. I needed to know that life was still happening. There, in the hospital, I didn't have to try and remember how to wipe her down. Someone came in. A stranger. They lifted the sheet.

At some point, I imagined, Micah and I would call hospice. I couldn't picture anyone bathing me. Then there was that movie about the Japanese family picking through the ashes with chopsticks, removing the family member's bones. A sacred ritual. I watched it while Micah slept. I told her about it later and she was devastated by the idea. I couldn't imagine love like that.

The living room began to fill with people. A spontaneous visit, from uninvited family. Micah held the screen door open. Siler had his arms out wide and was hollering, descending onto those who she'd welcomed inside. First there was one child, and then another two elderly women nearly identical, a third child, and then Sonya, Siler's second wife.

"Well, I think we're all here," Sonya said, pressing her palms against her heart and surveying the room. "Wait, where's my sister? And the baby?"

As if on cue, a woman stepped past the front door, which Micah was still diligently holding. The woman wore a red fedora and matching red lipstick, and a baby's head bobbed above a giant shawl wrapped around her torso. The family's laughter was incredible. The wildness of it. They couldn't stop laughing. Chatter bounced off the walls. The children, boys, all three of them, and still small, dribbled invisible balls through the house. The older women wore printed dresses with pleats, the hems of which covered their knees. They held their elbows, twisted the rings on their fingers. Sonya's hair, in two braids down to her waist, hung from the scarf she'd tied to her head. Micah must not have had the appropriation talk with her.

Sonya's father was from Mexico and her mother was from one of the nearby Indian pueblos, or her mother was from Mexico and her father was from some place, anyway, where they danced and had feasts. "You'll have to come to the dances," she'd said. "And remember the feast days." When I heard this repeated, first by Siler, and then by Micah, I nodded. I had no idea what it meant. What was the name of that place? A polysyllabic name bursting with vowels.

"This is for you," Sonya said. "From my mother."

She offered me a centerpiece made of corn stalks. The kernels were red and blue. Husks fanned above in a display of simple beauty that made me ache. This was not feed corn from the Midwest.

I was still in the same clothes—running pants and a sundress—that I'd been wearing since yesterday morning. I wanted to smile. I really did.

Micah thanked them all and placed the corn on the table. Everyone stopped to watch her.

"That's the perfect place," Siler said and thanked his mother-in-law for it, called it a blessing. There was more laughter, patting of hands, and side-hugs and Siler kissing Sonya.

I stood back, watching, as if I'd already become a ghost. I felt a warm tickle on my hand and almost slapped it away until I realized the youngest boy, Micah's brother, whose name I couldn't remember, was reaching for me.

"Where's the rabbits?" he said.

Within a half hour, they began leaving as quickly as they had appeared, parading toward the cars parked in the driveway and along the street. Micah trailed along. When I asked her where she was going, she said, "Family stuff," and turned her back to me. I wondered who, one day, she would claim. Who would claim her.

When the last car disappeared, I went straight for my bedroom. I pulled off the sundress and the running pants. I pushed the curtains from the double doors. Under the sheet, I lay diagonal across the mattress. As I felt my eyelids droop, I thought I saw the young man with the hat crawling around on the ground, arranging traps.

It was snowing. I remember that much because even as my mother pointed to the tracks, they disappeared. They were so small, more weight on the hind feet, so those made deeper, longer-lasting shapes. The rifle she carried was the same her mother had carried. Light and with hardly any kick, she'd told me in the days preparing for when it would be my turn to learn to use it. I remember how quiet it was, despite my feet dragging through the drifts. I remember the warmth of her body when she stood still and I leaned against her, how soft and strong she was under all her layers of wool. I held onto the Thermos and waited like she waited. Our breath, dancing plumes in the air.

She placed the rifle in my hands. She said, "I'm right here with you. We'll do it together." Even with my hat pulled down, I could feel the warmth of her whisper against my ear. I could feel the force of her finger on mine.

A blur. A tail. Sudden stillness. I felt her finger pressing mine firmly against the trigger.

I carried the rabbit home, not by the tail, as she instructed me, but cradled in my arms, its tail dangling. Lighter than I ever imagined.

In the bath that evening, after making the water extra warm, she praised me. "A woman who knows how to feed herself is a woman who will live forever."

"Can't you just feed me?" I said. I didn't want to be a woman who lived forever.

She rocked me to sleep that night, even though I was too old for that. I dreamt of its open mouth, which I'd stared into the whole walk back home. The teeth, curved and amber-stained, the long, narrow flap of tongue.

It was twilight when I woke. I couldn't tell where the clanging was coming from—inside or out? The bright red sticks on the alarm clock seemed to pulse. I couldn't make sense of the time. A figure moved near the sliding glass doors. The motion detector lights flicked on. I wrapped the sheet around me and managed to stand, too quickly at first, which meant losing my balance, falling back on the bed. The room tilting as I planned my second approach to standing, slower. My throat was desperate for water.

It took me a while to understand what I was seeing. I counted five wire-cage traps in the yard. When my eyes focused, I made out three with rabbits in them. The other two were empty and turned upside down. Micah had a rock, and was beating it against another latch. I could imagine how troubled the rabbit was, being caught, the noise, the light.

I poked my head out the door. "Are you trying to scare it to death?" I said.

"I can't get it open." Her voice was shrill. She was crying.

"It shouldn't be that difficult," I said, sitting down on the ground next to her. "It's just a rabbit trap." The rabbit was quivering with fear. The air was surprisingly cool, given how hot it'd been earlier. The sheet around me seemed to weigh as much I as did. I had to pull and tug and tuck it to keep it close to me. "You know it's for their own good, don't you?"

"I need to set them free," she said. The rock in her hand was oddly shaped, like a heart but pointed at one end, knife sharp. "Just show me how to do it."

"Micah, it's only a matter of time."

"Please, Mom." Her head fell into my lap as she cried harder. "Please."

I rested a hand on the back of her neck, and with the other, I undid the latch. It was much less complicated than she made it out to be. The rabbit didn't sprint away. It continued to shake, shifting its weight forward, slightly forward, then settling in again. We crawled over to the other traps and released those latches as well. It took time, but the rabbits ended up against the fence line under the bushes. A clump of them. Temporary refuge. I lay on the ground, the dirt and stiff grass pricking my skin, the sheet shrouding me. Micah knelt close by. I could hear her sniffling. With her head back, she searched the heavens. The stars painfully bright. No moon. All the traps turned upside down.

Mercury Was There
Libby Flores

Y LIFE WAS A MORSEL AT THE TIME. I WAS always looking at the doors of restaurants and bars instead of the face across from me. The light coming in: a silhouette, a promise. I was divorced, I told people. Making plans felt silly, pathetic even. But I did anyway, as friends said, as an "exercise."

My truck still ran. The house still moaned on every third step. I mowed our lawn—something Meg used to do. When I couldn't cross a room without blackening the bottoms of my feet, I managed to sweep. I missed the screen door slamming and fresh sheets on Sundays. The first year, a few kind ladies in town sent a cleaning woman who left well paid, but the rooms still untouched. The tomatoes went wild, ripened, split open, and then dropped, unpicked.

When I went to pick up my mail they still wanted to sell her life insurance or a new summer wardrobe. Instead of throwing the junk in the trashcan I set hers in a pile where she used to open it on the kitchen table. I inherited her debt, but I knew how little it mattered. I'd been paying to love her for years and now seeing out her Mastercard bill was just the tax. On Fridays, a trip to the PO box in town and finding her name printed there saved me a little. A part of her was still heading to me and I was still driving her home. Gissup is a small town in northern California and it was not her first choice. My job kept us there. When Meg met me in college she had ideas about how to change things. And all she needed was a masters degree. Instead of getting that degree, she took on a small town's education system. She watched me plan small parks and open lakeside camping grounds. There were cities that could have used her guts. But then, there was always someone who wanted her. That was the kind of woman she was.

We used to walk down to the stores after our coffee on Sundays. Just to look at things through the windows. She loved interior design and we'd stop and talk about what she liked in each display. Linen pillows, midcentury chests, and side tables clear of clutter—as they never are in life. We couldn't afford much. The glass separated us. In its shine on sunnier days I'd admire the two of us before we got close—her in a long dress, some flowery thing, and our hands clasped. My body was leaner then and my shirts were always clean.

When it was my turn to take out the trash I'd lift the lid and drop in the waste of our lives, even her scraps were not that heavy. I'd start to turn back, but pause. My gaze would hold at our house. The living room glowing warm orange and the sound of whatever record she'd put on to wash the dishes to— drifting out. We rented, but it felt like ours. With my head tilted up, right over the Bradleys' chimney, you could see Mercury shining like a porch light left on. Whether or not the moon was bright, Mercury was there.

It wasn't long till she started to get cramps in her legs. The shaking was the worst. It embarrassed her most. I still admired her spine—the thing holding her together. She'd try to be mean, lash out, but it was useless. She was angry at it. I was too. On some holiday or anniversary, I decided to make her pancakes. There was little cooking happening anymore. I watched videos and read up. Just like my practice exams for my landscaping license. I purchased the natural vanilla and bread flour. Pancakes are simple things to make, most say. We'd been using trays for her meals and I balanced the hot disks one on top of the other and butter nestled in between. OJ and water sloshing as I crossed the hall—her pills getting soaked from the spill. I walked into our bedroom, or by then her room really. She'd tried to comb her hair unsuccessfully and was weeping at the dropped brush near the bed. Her useless hands unable to grab it.

I'd forgotten the syrup. And without that, the

pancakes were just bready circles. It was comforting what her brown eyes could let me know. Schmuck, they said. My mistake made her forget the brush, me the syrup, and that was enough.

That breakfast was the last thing I made her. That night we slept as I dreamt of her tan body darting around thin trees at night almost in a dance, headlights reflecting off her thighs, a rabbit running back toward the swamp where she was raised.

At the beginning of our relationship, she wasn't mine—completely. She was living with a man off campus whose name she rarely mentioned. For about six months, she was always leaving. Leaving my apartment, leaving the city for out-of-town trips with his family, leaving to get eggs and not able to return. The sound of her keys rattling and her boots being zipped up years after we were together caused me panic.

We never really fought about it. Her leaving was an unspoken agreement. No matter how long our afternoons were, how much I made her laugh (she'd often laugh so hard she'd sneeze), I knew what I was getting. At this point I started to love her, but at the end of the day or weekend I'd have to let her go. Of course, eventually, the other man lost. I finally got his name. Sam—a man who suspected nothing and gave everything to Meg. He proposed to her and that was what finally made her leave. She cradled that guilt for years. Once after a bit of wine she told me that for nine months she'd wake up early and move his Sunday paper from the curb to his welcome mat.

Seven summers ago, I caught up with her one

night at a bar on a snaking back road off of I-90. It was the Fourth of July. She was supposed to be out with some friends. It had been so long since she'd left the house. I'd followed her to the bar to assure her safety. Holiday traffic and all. That's what I told myself. Truth was, since her diagnosis she was teetering on something all the time. It could be a bout of laughter or a sudden ambition to clean the garage, but it came in wallops of extremes. I'd hold the mop; I told myself. This is when men get tougher.

I'd watched them leave a bar together. Watched as this new stranger stuck his finger into one of the belt loops of her jeans. A move that made me jump a little, jostling my table. Somewhere I'd admired the move—the boldness of it, the fresh stupidity of it. She had met up with a few friends, but when they saw the two of them getting on they left in that way that women know how to leave. I had embarrassed myself in a lame disguise, my baseball cap, an old wind-breaker she wouldn't recognize, my posture a hunch. Our town hosted three main bars and on a Friday the Whiskey Tip was busy and unusually full. The night when interlopers appeared from neighboring cities, and to top it off it was the Fourth. I grabbed a seat in the back booth, the ones made for two. There was newer staff to cushion the holiday crowds so no "Hi Wal" or asking about the business.

My windshield had speckled bird shit across it and worse, on the inside, her obscured handprints from a day when she tried to take her bandana and clean it. I kept saying, It's outside, Meg, it's outside! What remained looked like desperate gestures to escape. Fingers in frenzy on the edges of my eye line. On a different day, this would've resembled a preschool hand painting. I kept forgetting to clean it.

I guess I understood. Her diagnosis new: a horrible thing waiting. A woman stamped with expiration. Her body was still together then, in control, not vibrating away from her. And he was someone who didn't know. A gift.

The back of his car said plenty. A dirty vehicle, an Acura at least ten years old. One aged bumper sticker I saw when my headlights hit it just so: a local mayoral-candidate campaign and expired tags.

It's the mornings when you can see where the love lies. The languid hope lingering, the smell of coffee, her long legs in terry-cloth shorts, and somewhere on my cluttered bedstand a cup used to appear, the cream still swirling in it—the light encapsulating the dark. He was a steady driver so no sudden stops. His rear window was dusty and slightly tinted. I'd know the back of Meg's head anywhere and I still couldn't make it out. I was thinking by now he'd graduated from a belt loop to a crotch seam. The last thing I drank in the bar, bourbon straight, was burning in my gut. A reminder that I'd skipped dinner to find something I did not want to know.

A van pulled between us with one of those dumb illustrations showing the family in stick figures, even the dog represented. I swerved to make sure they were still there, that silver Acura license plate not yet memorized.

He turned fast and sharp, something Meg would hate. She detested that kind of driving unless she was doing it. I thought of a bad joke then: what kind of man follows his wife? Well, what kind of wife?

So there we were barreling down a smaller road, fields of strawberries either side of it, dust picking up behind them, lights beaming brighter through the haze. Heading to his house maybe. This wasn't a lookout area and the fireworks were going to be south not north this year. The road changed to gravel. Their windows were open; her arm appeared outstretched and her thin fingers traced the air like a conductor. It was a cool evening for the Fourth. I still held back my boot over the gas, coasting a bit then pressing down, lifting it again like a compress. I stayed just far enough behind unnoticed, or it could be that to the two of them inside, that Acura was all there was. I'd come this far to see how much she wanted to undo.

She'd taken to reading her weekly horoscope. It was a different truth she wanted. One afternoon I dropped her at a tarot reader's house. I say house because putting a neon hand in your window does not make it a business. Honestly: I would have driven her anywhere. When I picked her up she was quiet but smiling and when I asked her what the woman said she put her arm around me and whispered, her voice breaking —I won't choke and don't forget to close the garage door at night. The doctor said she was lucky to catch it so early. I didn't know medical practitioners were allowed that word.

When I first asked her to marry me we'd been

dating a year. College was over and we'd combined our stuff in a small apartment in Santa Cruz. How I did it doesn't matter. But people ask. It was after dinner on one of our walks. No ring. Just a question. One of the most anxiety-inducing questions a man can ask. She said nothing for a long time. Then she grabbed my hand and squeezed it like a thank you. But didn't say yes. At the time, that singular moment held enough promise that I allowed the ambiguity.

I can only assume it was his house and that he must've been in the strawberry business. A one-story nothing that needed work. Concrete foundation and a roof cratering. They didn't get out of the car. The Acura stopped and she drew her hand back in the window. I parked across the road and watched as he cut his lights.

We wouldn't know then that a nurse would come in and loud equipment would live near our bed. That you have to decide when it's time to go on breathing machines and that the worst fear of the disease for the patient is choking on your own tongue. That we'd never buy that coffee table or marble coasters because being sick is expensive—more expensive than anything that was on the other side of those glass windows.

A security light clicked on and the passenger door opened—those legs slipped out. Something that sounded like "Jessie's Girl" was coming from the car. The notes echoed out of weak speakers that made me think of ice melting too far down in a drink. The headlights turned back on and he came out of the car, tilting back a fifth of something brown. He threw the bottle down and she was already laughing so hard that she was wiping her eyes. The lights shone through her white shirt and her arms so long, then, so strong still, waved over her head then side to side. She started to pull on it, teasing it out of her jeans. Each time it rose a little higher above her stomach on that dusty stage. He leaned on his car door taking in the last of the song and then he started his first steps toward her.

What indeed can you call a man who wears jeans that look like slacks? I thought, What if I crossed that road and caused the disease to speed up—all that adrenaline in her body. Irrational, I know. I imagined her looking up from her dance, her eyes dropping the laughter they held moments before, her shirt falling back into place. Even then, a small part of me hated to disappoint her. I turned my engine on.

It was then I could see her gaze, past his sloppy gait, into the cabin of my truck. For a month it had squealed when it started up—a neglected belt that needed attention. We had bigger fish. He paid no mind to it. To her it was a sound she not only knew but had embarrassed her on countless occasions, pulling out of grocery store lots, movie theaters, and once picking her up from a baby shower when it had reached such a pitch that we fought the whole way home. She knew.

Most understand that just as women are taught to cross their legs, men are always supposed to know what to do. There she was out of my reach again. Out there on that summer night with this stranger, I'd witness one of her last bright volleys. She didn't choke after all. I did.

I stayed to watch the scene. Their heads tilted up when the first firework of the night went. Its dandelion burst I could see in my rearview over the strawberries. Fucker had planned it right.

And when I drove home from work today I saw those shitty stands on the side of the road selling bottle rockets and Black Cats. The sellers have aged, but they're still handing out free smoke bombs with purchase. Then it begins. I'll hear them start up weeks ahead of the holiday. Mostly kids at first, but it gets worse from there. I find myself under our comforter, like a dog, waiting it out.

It was a last-minute decision, but when her parents and I were selecting her clothes I slipped the ring on a thin string, our tightrope, and asked the mortician to place it around her neck. Maybe I wanted to finally have something on her.

I never looked up at the sky that night, but I heard the pops coming at a greater speed. I sat there in the driver seat and watched the colors reflect on the siding of his house and when she stepped closer to him, I saw her shirt and face turn shades of red, then blue, then white again.

A Place Called Beautiful

Jane Hammons

WHEN YOU LIVE IN A TOWN LIKE VLAN, AND it is not much of a town, you must look far and wide for a place that is pretty enough for a picnic with your family and friends. If you should find a spot in the dry scrub and yellow grass, don't go so far as to take visitors from out of town there, expecting them to marvel at its beauty. It is unlikely they will share your view. But down by the river there is a place called beautiful, and if you find it, you will not be alone. The water is the color of a well-worn slate, the earth red clay. In winter when covered with a brittle layer of frost, you will seldom see another soul out there. Bent twigs of mesquite along the river path, barely visible impressions upon the near frozen ground and the slight muddying of otherwise undisturbed waters are the only signs that someone has come before you. Few appreciate this beauty. Hondo Duggins and Estrellita Serna were two. Before the first snow fell and ice formed on the surface of the water they buckled up and took a drive to the bottom of the river.

Hondo and Estrellita were one year out of high school and still hanging around town like kids do when they don't go off to college or out to the oil fields. Hondo was a busboy at Benny's. Estrellita was a student at the Beauty College. Their absence was noted with silence for fear that merely pronouncing their names would disturb the quiet that had come since they had gone, which is exactly what happened once the strange woman arrived.

Plagued by dreams of hair—long twisting strands, short blunt clumps—she'd wake to find her auburn tresses decorating the pillow where she slept, the follicles black and dead. Her stylist assured her it was common in middle-aged women.

"I hardly qualify as middle-aged." The woman bristled at what was meant to be reassuring information.

The stylist did not respond. She didn't know the woman well, but she'd done her hair often enough to know she didn't want to do it again. She bestowed upon the woman her last tube of a homeopathic treatment her parents had made before they were forced to cease production because of their products' disturbing side effects. She took the tube of ointment from a drawer.

"Riovlan." The woman read from label. "What is it?"

"I don't know," said the stylist, and that was true enough. "But it works."

Following the directions on the tube, the woman massaged the ointment into her head for several nights. She didn't expect immediate results, but she also didn't expect to see a young couple appear next to her own image in the mirror as she sat at her vanity. Frightened by the hallucination, the woman immediately swore off the Riovlan and shoved it into a drawer. But the next morning, there were fewer strands of dead hair on her pillow. She attributed the ghostly images to her stress, and returned to the treatment regimen. Again the young man and the young woman appeared, even more clearly this time. Though concerned about her mental state, she could not help but note how handsome the man was, how beautiful the woman, what a perfect couple they made. Over the next few days, she saw them reflected everywhere she looked—the side view mirrors of cars in parking lots, puddles of water left by rain and even in the highly polished surface of the wide cleaver she used for chopping lettuce.

She interpreted the advent of the two youths as a sign she was meant to be part of a couple, so she flirted with inferiors at work and visited a dating website a couple of times before deeming the available male population of her town worthless. The ointment almost gone, her head full of hair, she dreaded the loss of her visitations as much as she had the appearance of dead follicles. The couple wiped her tears, stroked her cheek and ran their fingers through her hair until at last the woman got it. Their ministrations were an invitation. She wasn't meant to be part of just any couple. She was meant to join them. She consulted the tube of ointment that had summoned their appearance, noted where it was made, quit her job and closed up her apartment. Then she purchased a bus ticket to Vlan, a place few have dreamt of.

Upon arrival the woman appraised herself in the glass door of the bus station. She smoothed her skirt over her trim hips, tucked her soft white blouse into the tiny waistband of her skirt, then yanked her suitcase from the bottom of the pile on the luggage cart and headed down River Street to The Rio Inn, its metal sign beaten and battered by the sun and wind into the flat dull sameness of the rest of the town.

While the woman waited for the couple, she wandered out to the little kidney-shaped swimming pool where she admired herself for as long as she could stand the heat. In the evening, she'd walk along the dusty banks of the soggy creek that ran behind the inn. Covered by trickling water, bright ferns flourished beneath the surface. Fronds extending above the shallow water were dead, blackened by the sun. Reminded of her affliction, the woman took this as a clue and began visiting every beauty parlor, as they were still called, in Vlan. She asked questions about a young couple, describing Hondo and Estrellita perfectly. No one responded until finally Lupe Villanueva directed the woman to Velynda Ashcroft's Beauty College.

In the restful months that had passed since Estrellita's absence, Velynda Ashcroft had put the wicked girl out of her immediate thoughts. She became agitated when the redhead came into the Beauty

College asking questions about a girl who had once attended her college. Noting Velynda's distress, the woman knew she had found a source. She sat down in one of the many vacant chairs, freed her long hair from a tight French twist and requested a shampoo.

Velynda's hands tingled with the anticipation of getting her hands into that gorgeous hair. She tied a stiff plastic apron around the woman's neck and led her to a sink where she plunged her fingers into the auburn locks, shampooed and rinsed, shampooed and rinsed again as she talked about the frustration of teaching cosmetology to students who did not truly appreciate the science of beauty, did not comprehend the importance of the right haircut, professionally manicured nails, the correct moisturizer, foundation and lipstick.

Estrellita Serna. Velynda could not stop herself from saying the name, was such a student. She had not attended college to learn how to properly cut, comb, and curl, but only to pass the hours her boyfriend was at work. Estrellita refused to keep up her tuition payments. She stole beauty supplies. But worse, she had destroyed the reputation of the Beauty College.

Every fall Velynda and her students represented their profession in the County Fair Parade. And every fall since Marva Kunkel was thirteen years old, all the beauticians in Vlan had vied for the presence of her thick chestnut hair on their float. With the promise of a year's worth of styling and beauty products, Velynda had won Marva in last year's contest.

On the morning of the parade Velynda, Marva and all of the students gathered at the College to style

one another's hair. Only Estrellita was idle; she refused
to style her glossy black hair, letting it hang as always
straight to her waist. So Velynda assigned Estrellita
the task of turning Marva Kunkel's ponytail into long
symmetrical ringlets. But instead Estrellita cut it off
and ran shrieking triumphantly from the College,
waving the shimmering trophy as she went, leaving
Marva with an unattractive ducktail protruding from
the back of her head.

Though in a state of shock Velynda and her
students were determined to go on with the show.
Velynda surrounded herself with her sniffling, nail-
biting students and rode center stage, having whipped
her hair into a hurried beehive that collapsed half way
down River Street. The tale of Estrellita's assault on
Marva spread quickly along the twelve blocks from
North to South River where the parade ended. Towns-
people booed and hissed at the Beauty College float as
it rolled past, its black tires disguised as pink sponge
curlers.

Filled with compassion for the shorn Marva
Kunkel and repelled by Estrellita's behavior, the
woman doubted it was Estrellita she sought. But to be
certain she asked for the address of Estrellita's family.

Weary from washing, combing out and blasting
every bit of natural wave out of the woman's hair with
a powerful blow-dryer, Velynda didn't think to ask why
she wanted it but trudged to the shoebox where she
kept the delinquent file. After giving the woman directions to the Serna's house, she closed up shop. Overhead small dark clouds, clenched like fists, beat upon

the glaring face of the sun. Blinded by jagged flashes of lightning that ripped open the sky in a sudden thunderstorm, Velynda dashed madly across the street to her usual parking space in front of Primm's Pharmacy just as Tad Ostermann sped down toward her, an hour late for a date with his girlfriend Marva Kunkel. He didn't see Velynda and hit her hard. She flew several feet into the air before landing in the back of his truck. Her spine snapped, Velynda died quickly, splayed out in the bed of manure Tad had planned to spread on his mother's lawn.

Sip Drang, sole reporter for *The Vlan Daily Witness*, was in the pharmacy purchasing travel-size toiletries to take on his annual vacation, keeping a journal from which he'd write his popular "Great American Sights" column. Folks in Vlan don't get out of town much, so he used "GAS" as a way to educate them about the larger world. Sip saw the entire incident and supported Tad's claim that it was a terrible accident though the town gossips would call it an act of revenge.

Meanwhile the woman walked toward the Serna's small brick house on Sunset Ave. According to Velynda, Estrellita was a great beauty, but there was little evidence that she had inherited her looks from the woman who answered the door, Mrs. Serna appearing wrinkled and worn beyond any reasonable effect of time. She stood firmly in the doorway and told the woman that Estrellita had probably run off with her boyfriend, Hondo Duggins. Then she shut the door.

The woman walked a few blocks to Benny's diner where she assumed she'd find an intact phonebook in the indoor phone booth. Three Duggins were listed. She called each of them asking for Hondo. The first swore at her; the second number was no longer in order. On her third call, she found a woman named Modine who owned up to being the boy's mother, gave her directions, and invited her over.

Modine Duggins had plenty of things to worry about. The disappearance of Hondo was not one of them. She counted that among her few blessings. Her husband had recently run off with another woman, and she'd just had a phone conversation with her daughter, Nodell, who said she had found a lump on her right breast. But she welcomed the woman into her home anyway. She hauled out the family scrapbook to show the woman a picture of Hondo but ended up showing her a collection of newspaper articles about Nodell's short-lived career as a faith healer.

After a few reported successes, Nodell had attempted to cure Mrs. Russell Palmeyer of arthritis. When she grabbed the cane from the old woman's hand and commanded her to dance before God, Mrs. Palmeyer had fallen flat on her face, breaking an arm and cracking a cheekbone. Nodell had been so shamed by Sip Drang's damning articles in *The Witness* that she moved out of town.

Hondo? Modine turned to his section and showed the woman clippings about her son's numerous arrests for fighting, drunk driving, and vandalism. She'd quit reading them but dutifully continued to clip and paste them into the family chronicle. Just what was the

nature of the woman's business with him anyway,
Modine wanted to know.

The woman told Modine how she had been summoned to Vlan. She made clear she was not certain
Hondo was the man of her dreams. He certainly
resembled the pictures of the boy in Modine's album,
but she was having a hard time reconciling the love
she had felt from him with the deeds of Hondo
Duggins.

For the first time in her life, Modine Duggins
had not a single word to say. She thought maybe the
woman had escaped from an asylum and directed her
to the door. Then she left a message for Nodell out
at the trailer park north of town where she had set
up business. *PALMS READ HERE* the white board
with a big red hand on it announced to travelers who
ventured down the highway. When she finally returned
her mother's call and heard the story of the redhead's
visit, Nodell claimed that she had recently dreamt of
Hondo dead in a watery grave. She felt destined to
meet the woman who might have more information.
She had a few appointments, but she promised to be
home early the following day.

As eager as Nodell was to reach Vlan so was the
woman eager to leave it. The youth she dreamt of
could not be born of these ugly women in this ugly
town. She checked the bus schedule. One last night
in Vlan then she would return to her apartment and
begin looking for work. The very thought of updat-
ing her resume gave her a headache. She'd never had
an easy time finding or keeping a job. Not even an-

gry that she'd given no notice only a few days ago, her supervisor had simply escorted her to the door. Feeling foolish, she began packing her bag.

The woman arrived at the bus station early the following morning, purchased her ticket and was the first to board. She hadn't slept well the previous night. Praying that the couple would come to her rescue, she tossed and turned until it was time for her to get up. As the bus pulled out of the station, she closed her eyes and fell into a deep sleep. The young man and woman surfaced in her murky dream, and she began to choke and gasp for air.

Sip Drang, who had given his statement to the police along with a list of telephone numbers where he could be reached, was seated directly across the aisle from the woman. He jerked her up out of her seat, positioned himself behind her and performed a quick Heimlech on her.

Infuriated and not the least bit grateful to find herself in the arms of the chubby bald man, the woman shoved Sip away. Sip let the bus driver take over. He was on vacation after all, and he had only recently witnessed the demise of Velynda Ashcroft. He didn't need any more trauma in his life. He'd handed the writing of Velynda's obituary off to his friend Lupe Villanueva who covered *The Witness* for him when he was on vacation. He wasn't sorry he'd miss Velynda's funeral. Next to Nodell Duggins, Velynda was one of his least favorite people. The two of them had taunted him, wondering how someone so homely and fat could be the son of such a beautiful woman, however crazy she might have been. They'd flirt with him and then reject him, jerking him around like a yoyo.

Because the woman wouldn't stop shrieking about a boy and a girl she needed to find, the bus driver decided to take her to the hospital in Vlan. He swung the bus around, nearly running Nodell Duggins off the road.

The ER doctor examined the woman, asking her questions she found entirely too personal. Had this ever happened before? Was there someone the hospital should contact? What kind of medications was she on?

The woman declared she was on no medication except for the Riovlan she'd been using for the past month.

"Riovlan?"

The woman took the empty crinkled tube from her purse and gave it to him. "It's made here. I'd like to buy more if you know where I can find it. I wasn't able to locate the name of the business in the phone book."

The doctor examined the tube. "La Oscuridad, Inc. Not familiar with it. *Massage into scalp nightly*," he read the directions aloud. "Have to be careful what you put in your head." He chuckled at his joke, but got no response from the woman. He handed the tube back to her.

"I didn't put them there. They came to me."

Puzzled, the doctor stared at the woman. Then decided not to ask what she meant. "I can give you something for anxiety."

"Anxiety?" The woman scoffed at the suggestion she suffered from that condition. "A little hair loss," she said. "That's the only health problem I've ever had in my life."

"What you experienced on the bus sounds like a panic attack." The doctor explained his diagnosis.

"I was drowning." Only in the moment she spoke those words did she understand the vision she'd had on the bus. Catching sight of her rather disheveled appearance in the towel dispenser, she smoothed her hair and left with renewed determination. Somewhere, in dark waters, the couple awaited her arrival.

When you ask people in Vlan about bodies of water, as the woman began to do, they are most likely to tell you about their ditches, tanks, and reservoirs. They might quote you the cost of their new pump or tell you how much they paid to have a well dug. If they mention the river, it will only be to dismiss it. Fishing is poor—mud cats and carp. It is not consistently wide or deep enough for boating or water-skiing. There are no shade trees, so in summer if you are tempted to go there for a swim, you are likely to find yourself alone.

Teenagers go to the river for precisely this reason. There is nothing to do, and they can rest assured there will be no babies or old people to bother them. As they mature and feel the need to find entertainment outside themselves, they'll drive the thirty miles to Bottomless Lakes. Many of them just keep going. That's how Nodell Duggins explained the lack of youth in Vlan to the woman who found her annoying but tolerated her because Nodell let her use her car while she worked.

She was eager to provide assistance in the search for Hondo and Estrellita, sure that her recent visions would lead to their location and restore her reputation as healer and visionary.

Night after night, the woman was drawn to the cliffs above the river. She parked near the bridge at a turnout in the highway called Scenic Spot. The Spot is where high school kids go to make out. Encased in their automobiles, they find the privacy they long for even though most nights the Spot is about as private as the laundromat on a Saturday morning.

The woman had spent enough time at Scenic Spot to know that if she sat there long enough she would see at least one shooting star. When she saw the pair falling in perfect unison and watched their arc disappear into the river below, she knew she had found her destination.

She fixed in her mind the place where the two stars had fallen and drove back to town. She noted a dirt road that led away from the highway to the river. She was confident that in the light of the following day she would be able to find the place. She was eager to return to the Rio Inn and check her map of the area, but first she had to meet Nodell at Benny's for what the woman knew would be the last time. As soon as the sun rose, she intended to return to the river. And she intended to return alone.

Sip Drang thanked Lupe again for picking him up at the bus station and waved to her as she backed out of his front drive. From her he'd learned Nodell

Duggins was back in town, and that for the past week she'd been stirring things up with a story about how she and a psychic were looking for the bodies of Hondo and Estrellita who had been visiting them both in dreams and visions.

Sip quickly unpacked, put away his clothing and toiletries without his usual concern for neatness. Then he donned the Panama hat he had purchased in Baton Rouge and left the house. Eager to learn more about Nodell and her psychic sidekick, Sip pressed the gas pedal to the floor and sped toward Benny's where everyone was always willing to talk.

When Sip entered Benny's he was shocked to find that Nodell was something called a dinner hostess. As Benny's had never before had a hostess, he correctly assumed that Nodell had managed to create a job for herself. She turned a cold shoulder to Sip, who seated himself at the coffee counter where he was greeted by those who awaited his return with stories of their own to tell: a new grandchild; a two-headed snake found out on someone's ranch; Bervin Fall's prize Longhorn had died.

Knowing Nodell, Sip was prepared for just about anything but he was not prepared to see the woman he'd Heimliched on the bus plaster a fake smile on her face and wave cheerfully at Nodell, inviting her to sit at her booth. Curious, Sip got up to inquire after the woman's health. Fine, was all the woman said and dismissed him brusquely.

Nodell shot Sip a wicked smile, pleased with the discomfort her new friend had caused him. She slid into the seat across from the woman and explained loud enough for all to hear that Sip used *The Witness* to spread malicious gossip. The woman, who was beginning to get on Nodell's nerves, seemed preoccupied and did not respond to her. Nodell ground her teeth. In the short time they'd been sitting together, the woman had admired herself in the window and had even managed to get a quick look at herself in the underside of the waitress's shiny metal tray. She was using a water glass as a mirror and applying fresh lipstick. Nodell needed a break. She told the woman she'd be unable to drive her around the next day.

The woman again said merely, "Fine." She explained she needed to catch up on her beauty sleep anyway and the sooner she started the better. She left Nodell sitting in her booth and walked back to The Rio Inn.

Sip finished the last bite of pie, wished everyone good evening, then drove to the Rio Inn and parked across the street. There he waited, imagining headlines, lead sentences, and the Who What When Where Why and How of his next big story, another revealing the chicanery of Nodell Duggins and whoever the redhead was.

Inside her room, the woman took a pen and blackened the road on the map that would lead her to the place in the river. Early the next morning she paid the desk clerk twenty dollars for the use of his car. She drove out of Vlan, past the places that had become familiar to her. Cheerful and feeling at home, she even waved to the boys on a hay truck. Sip Drang, who followed at a discreet distance, had a sick feeling about where she was headed.

As the woman drove along the river road, she watched the water grow faster and deeper with every mile. She stopped near the place where the water runs purple and gray. She got out of the car and made her way down the river path, creeping in and out between the cacti and cholla, until she reached the water's edge.

The river licked at the tips of her open-toed pumps and invited her in. Caressed by the current, she walked into deeper water. Lulled by the swirl between her thighs, the woman shivered with desire.

From a ridge, Sip watched. He would never forget the day that he and some other youngsters—Nodell and Velynda among them—had taken a large wooden raft out to the river in the back of his father's pick-up. When they put the raft in the water, Nodell told him about the contest they were going to have. What she described hadn't seemed like much of a challenge. In fact, it seemed like the kind of dumb thing Nodell and her friends would think was an accomplishment. They'd take the raft out to the deep water. Each person would swim the length of the raft while those aboard timed the swimmer. The fastest person won. Though he didn't expect to win, he knew he could swim from one end to the other. Sip slid off the back end with a confident splash. As he swam beneath it, the raft grew longer, the water darker.

Sip remembered swimming for what seemed an eternity, surfacing in the belief that he had surely reached the end of the raft, bumping his head each time on its underside. Logic told him to swim to the side of the raft and away from it. But his pride and the river's dark current kept him paddling pointlessly forward.

Weary of the constant thump thump of Sip's head beneath the raft as he tried to rise for air and the fear that they might actually cause him to drown, one of the boys dove in and rescued Sip as he descended into the muddy arms of the river bottom. Later everyone laughed as they roasted marshmallows around a campfire, telling him that as he swam, they had paddled, negating any progress he made. They had played the trick on others who had all been smart enough to simply swim away from the raft once they began to tire. No one had ever been as dumb as Sip Drang. "No wonder your mother left you behind," he could hear Velynda Ashcroft saying again, "you're not just fat, you're stupid, too." He let them laugh and said nothing about the seductive force that had pulled him deeper and deeper into the river.

Sip scrambled down the river path and plunged in after the woman. When he saw her disappear, he took a deep breath and dove after her, grabbing her by the hair, and to his horror ripped it easily away.

Her lungs filling with water, the woman clutched her bald head in humiliation. She sank into the purple water where she saw Hondo's dirty black car. Decayed flesh dripped from Hodo and Estrellita's bodies. Tiny fish swam in and out of their eye sockets. Tendrils of green algae and moss flowed from their mouths. Their noses were plugged with debris and mud. Dozens of

Styrofoam wig stands bobbed about in the back seat. A blank-faced hollow chorus, they jeered at her. Angry at their betrayal, she pulled at the door handle, but it gave way in her hands. They were beyond her reach. An old catfish with sickly pink eyes circled the woman, jutting back and forth between her legs, tickling her with its whiskers. It gave the woman one last scaly caress before she slid beneath Hondo's car and settled behind one of the tires.

Sip walked back to the ridge, his soggy sneakers leaving damp impressions upon the ground. When he looked inside the car the woman drove to the river, he saw the map inside her large open purse. Next to it, something caught his eye—a shiny flattened tube decorated with a purple snakelike figure. Something familiar about it filled him with dread. He retrieved the tube and discovered it was what he suspected. Riovlan, made by La Oscuridad, Inc., his parents' old company. Riovlan was just one of their many products made from the red clay he stood upon mixed with the waters of Rio Oscuro that flowed past him as well as plants native to the area. So many people complained about the sickening side effects of their homemade remedies that they had eventually gone bankrupt and out of business. Sip's mother took his little sister with her to live among a group of Wiccans, leaving Sip behind with his father, who became a goat farmer for a few years before dying from an undiagnosed stomach ailment. Sip put the tube in his pocket. It had been a long time since he'd thought about his family. He credited his career in journalism to their talk about

magic and cures and spells. Disgusted by their supersti-
tions, not to mention the harm they'd done him and his
sister, using them as guinea pigs for their concoctions,
he'd turned to facts.

But he'd lived in Vlan long enough to understand
that there were things he could not explain. He put
the empty tube of Riovlan in his pocket, drove to his
house, changed his clothes, and went to Benny's for an
early lunch.

Sip ate his omelet slowly, waiting until Nodell had
no one to seat, no kids to boost into booster chairs,
no customer to chat with. Then he took a deep breath
and approached the hostess station, which was just a
TV tray that Nodell had brought in to sit behind.
Before she could begin insulting him, he apologized
for the harsh words he'd used in reporting on Mrs.
Palmeyer's accident. Mouth agape, Nodell stared at
him with the deep green eyes that had so captivat-
ed him in his youth. He fought the impulse to fidget
like a lovesick boy. He told her about his new column
for *The Witness*, "VIP: Vlan's Important People." If she
wanted, she could be his first subject. In it, she could
respond to the faith-healing fraud article if she chose
to. Nodell listened, chewing on her already chapped
lips. She was suspicious but interested.

When she told Sip she'd consider it, he acted
grateful. "Don't wait too long. I need the interview
by tomorrow." He took a peppermint candy from a
glass dish and unwrapped it slowly. "My second choice
is that new woman—the redhead." He popped the
peppermint into his mouth.

"She can't be a VIP," Nodell protested, "she's not even from Vlan."

"Well," said Sip. "She seems to love the place, the way she drives all over the countryside. And let's face it, she's a knockout. A photo of her on the front page will sell a lot of papers."

"Fine. Tomorrow," said Nodell.

"I'll pick you up, and we'll drive out to the river. Real pretty this time of year."

Nodell snorted. "It's never pretty no time of year. I want my photo taken in front of my trailer." She held both of her palms out in front of her. "PALMS READ HERE."

"Your trailer isn't really in Vlan. We need a local background, especially for the launch story."

Determined to become the first VIP, Nodell agreed to the river.

"Four o'clock sharp. Maybe we'll catch a pretty sunset."

"Don't get any ideas, fat man," said Nodell.

"Strictly business." Sip cracked the peppermint between his teeth and left.

The next day Sip and Nodell made uncomfortable small talk—the only thing in common a history of dislike. Sip talked about his recent trip to Louisiana. Nodell described how to read the palm of a hand.

When Sip pulled up right next to the car the woman had driven to the river, Nodell hopped out, curious about who was there. When she looked inside, she recognized the familiar marked up map the woman had left on the seat. Nodell yanked the door open and grabbed it. "What are you and that crazy woman up to?" She waved the map in his face.

Sip played dumb. "I had no idea she'd be here." Casually he followed the path the woman had taken to the water. "Looks like she went this way.

Nodell scurried to catch up with him as he approached the water. "You have some crazy idea we're going to compete for VIP, for your attention. Dream on, you idiot." She grabbed Sip by the arm meaning to spin him around and unload a barrage of humiliating name-calling on him. She was surprised when he pulled her into the river behind him.

"She's waiting for you," he said.

Nodell recoiled at his touch, but as they tussled in the shallow water, she became excited by Sip's hands slipping up her skirt and down her blouse. He groped and grabbed trying to get a firm hold on her. They tumbled farther out into the river, losing their footing as the current grew stronger, the river deeper. Nodell got up on Sip's back and pushed him under. She held him down and beat on his bald head. Thump thump. She laughed, remembering the sound of his head bumping the bottom of the raft so long ago. She was surprised when Sip surfaced easily and tossed her off. He swam for the dark water. Determined to teach him another lesson Nodell slipped out of her skirt and swam after him, thinking he must have forgotten that she'd been the state 400-meter freestyle champ all four years in high school.

Sip was happy to see her taking the bait, but

the sight of a newly energized Nodell, her muscular legs churning the water, made him tired. He wasn't worried about the dark water. Twice he'd been caught in its current, and twice it had released its hold on him. He worried that he wouldn't have the stamina to lure her out to the deep water.

Just as Nodell reached him, she went down. She popped back up, her eyes wide in surprise. She yelled something at him before she went down again. When she surfaced the third time she flailed only briefly before she disappeared.

When he got to the shore, Sip picked up the map Nodell had dropped along with her handbag and tossed them into the river. If their bodies were found, the people of Vlan would acknowledge a logical conclusion to the story they'd gossiped different versions of for the past couple of weeks. He sat down on the bank of the river and warmed himself against the flat sandstone rocks that layered the shore. He took off his shirt and let the heat of an early spring sun warm his flabby white belly. He saw the delicate blossoms quiver on the hardy cactus. He allowed the yellow grass to tickle his face and chest. He watched the fluffy white clouds separate, revealing the brilliance of a turquoise sky. Dark water coursed through his veins, and he called the place beautiful.

⟶

The Unremarkable Life of Mrs. Shin

Mark L. Keats

FTER THE BOMBS FELL FOR NINETY DAYS AND ninety nights—what would later be known as "Operation Insomnia"—Mrs. Shin, then known only as Kyung, somehow survived the devastation and eventual splitting of her country. When the bombing stopped and she awoke, she called to her mother and father, to her younger brother, but only silence returned. It wasn't long before she came upon their bodies, their home, pieces of her previous life. Her country was mountainous, but had she known what a desert looked like, she would have understood the devastation she now saw.

She did not cry in that moment because she understood something she should not have had to understand: that life, with all of its beauty, was also full of ugliness and silence. Pieces. She alone buried her family and marked their graves with many, many stones. Still, she did not cry. She moved.

She fled southward, and whenever she heard airplanes above took cover and expected to hear explosions and find more devastation. Over the days, she passed by many bodies, more desert, where once there were trees and lush rice fields, villages and life. She hadn't eaten in some time, but she kept moving. She kept moving until her legs gave way, until she felt the gravel scraping her knees, until she could not move anymore. She awoke to find herself looking at the horizon sideways, pieces of gravel and dirt clinging to her lips and cheek.

Somehow a local farmer, who had also survived, came upon her small body. He'd only recently buried his son and daughter, his wife. Now, he tried to bury this poor girl who looked no older than ten because he thought she was dead and that was the right thing to do. But he couldn't find the strength to dig another grave, so he covered her small body as best he could, then headed south until he finally succumbed to his injuries, wondering, if only briefly, in that final moment, where the girl he buried had come from, what she herself had seen.

But she coughed and woke up, spit out the dust and dirt that had collected in her mouth. She began removing the dirt and rocks. She tried to stand up, but she was too weak, and soon the sun began to set again.

"Hey, hey there," a voice said. She could barely open her eyes, and though she didn't yet understand English, she understood an important thing when finally she saw the man's eyes, blue, his friendly smile: she had been found, which meant, in so many ways, that she might survive. "*Mul*," she said. "*Mul*." The man gave her water, which stung the dryness of her mouth. But she drank as much as she could, with closed eyes. In a seminar decades later, she would learn that the very people who now helped her had dropped the bombs and split her country.

But, for now, though she was exhausted, she could finally rest. In the darkness, she heard the man speak more words she didn't yet understand. Then, other voices. Trucks. The smell of diesel. They moved south, past more bodies, many more unknown families among them, until they came to the city. Then, some-how, soon, she was flying. She kept her eyes closed, existed in a darkness that, if she concentrated, allowed her to see the outline of her previous life.

Somehow, as if all she had done was wake after a long interval, a fever perhaps, as if someone closed one door, then opened another, Mrs. Shin sits in a park in Maryland on a warm summer evening. Her grandson, Andrew, is by her side. He is five and has known only one home, one country. America. He laughs and runs and eats more than any other child she has ever seen. But she will always ask him, as she has always asked all of her children, now adults in the backyard eating and drinking and talking. "Are you hungry, did you eat?"

And her children, those boys, ate and ate, and they grew up to be tall and strong and with very few ques-tions about where their mother had come from. What had led her to immigrate. Why there were no relatives to visit or host. They grew up American; they spoke English (and sometimes Korean) and grew up with American holidays: Thanksgiving, Christmas, New Year's, Valentine's, the Fourth of July.

It has taken time to embrace the annual fireworks that now light up the sky every summer, that mark this country's independence, the homeland of her late husband, a historian. A man who loved to discuss the Battle of Baltimore, the Star-Spangled Banner. The cost of freedom.

She understood why the family dog would run and hide beneath their bed, would not come out until the sounds had long lost that energy, and even then, he seemed unsure until she coaxed him out, her scent a comforting salve. "Let him be," she'd told her children, of the dog, as she tells her grandson now with his.

"Look, Grandma," Andrew says, as fireworks fly upward, explode, and dissipate into the darkening sky. "Look, pretty."

She looks at him, then gives a little smile. "Yes, very pretty." But after the bright colors diminish, she studies the lingering smoke and smells the sulfur, and thinks of her brother and her parents, her homeland. A mountain made desert. She touches her grandson lightly upon his head, looks at him closely. The future. And she's reminded how loud life can be.

➤

Sargasso
Laura Lee Lucas

TOBY IS MARRIED TO LANA.

Lana is beautiful.

She is even more beautiful than she was when they were engaged and her name was Alana, more beautiful than she was when they first began to date and her name was Alaina.

Lana is so beautiful she comes home only one day a week, if that.

She appears on the doorstep laden with bags: sometimes shopping bags, filled with brand-new clothes; sometimes, grocery bags, filled with sumptuous treats. Life, for Lana, does not seem to consist so much of actual meals as of a parade of treats; many to be eaten with fingers from containers that frequently serve only one.

If the bags hold food, Lana gives them to Toby to put away. If they hold clothes, she carries them into the bedroom and puts them away herself.

When everything is sorted off into drawers and behind doors, Lana stands in the doorway of the bedroom, one hand on each side of the frame, dressed only in the slip that had been hidden beneath her dress, or perhaps in a négligée that she has just unfurled from a bag. She leans forward slightly, just enough for the shadow between her breasts to catch the light, and flare into gleaming skin.

Toby is drawn to her like a moth at moonrise. As he comes closer, she backs away, step for step, until she is standing with her back to the bed. Then she and Toby sink slowly into it, and the night disappears.

He never remembers the lovemaking itself. He returns to himself only afterward, lying next to Lana's sleeping form in the dark, feeling the power slowly ebbing from his veins, feeling the aches deep in his muscles.

In his presence, Lana never speaks a single word.

She sleeps with her back turned to him, one perfect shoulder dark against the creamy sheets.

In the morning, she is gone before the sun.

Toby wasn't sure when he first realized that there was something wrong with his marriage.

It might have been as he was shaving, razor poised to slice through white drifts of foam like a boat through storm waves.

It might have been a moment when he found his hand on the knob of the front door, and paused in confusion before releasing it.

But at some point, the feeling descended on him

that something in all this was wrong.

Something in *his marriage* was wrong.

Toby was confused.

The trouble grew.

Toby looked around the house and realized the furniture—drapes, carpets—were not his selections. No doubt they were Lana's. Surely he had paid—he was the husband, after all—but clearly she had chosen. Nothing was truly his, save for his clothes and a few items in the bedroom that predated their marriage: his high school yearbooks; two framed photographs of his parents; the old Boy Scout uniform and patches he kept in a box in the bottom dresser drawer. Sometimes he would sift through them and immerse himself in the memories of obtaining each one, their possession seeming to cement his presence.

There's nothing wrong with that, is there? he thought. Weren't men *supposed* to be more sentimental these days? In fact, weren't wives supposed to decorate the house? Maybe there was nothing wrong with any of it.

Toby's head began to hurt. He looked to his left, out of the picture window.

The bedroom was several stories up, with a lake view. The lake was a cloudy green. When the sun struck it just so, it glowed like a dream of the sea.

The sea.

Before the marriage, Toby had been an avid sailor. He'd spent every free moment hauling lines, touching up paint, taking weekend trips down the coast in one of his boats. The *Swift*, his favorite, had carried him up and down every mile of coastline close to his childhood home.

Toby couldn't remember the last time he had gone sailing. That seemed important.

What had happened to the boats?

He looked out to the gleaming lake. No boats glided upon its jade waters.

He wandered through the rooms, feeling vaguely silly. But there were no boats to be had in any of them.

One room was lined floor-to-ceiling with books, and before a fireplace a single leather chair and matching couch dyed a deep oxblood crouched on a heavy Persian carpet of gold darkening to honey brown.

Another room contained shelves and shelves of glass bottles in varying shapes and heights, with equally diverse contents. They held varicolored powders and liquids. Some appeared to contain rocks. Bugs had flown into a few empty vessels, and died—though, oddly, those were corked shut. A round, empty table sat exactly in the room's center.

There was a small chamber with a huge fireplace that ran the entire length of one wall. The opposite wall was completely covered with large cabinet doors. Toby pulled at the knobs.

They were all locked.

Surely the boats weren't in a closet.

In a room that was perfectly round, with windows looking out to the lake, Toby found charts of the sea.

More than charts—land maps, navigational charts, compasses, some older, some newer. They littered two large tables on either side of the central window and lurked in stacks all over the floor, snagging his bare feet if he turned too quickly.

There were no boats here either, of course, but . . .

Did Lana sail?

Toby tried to remember, really tried, and found that he didn't know.

What use is a room full of sailing charts, if you don't sail?

Toby ran out of the chart room, yanking the door shut.

He grabbed hold of the mahogany banister in the hallway with both hands and stood there for a moment, breathing shakily.

There was a strange feeling in his chest and head, as though his thoughts and blood were swirling together in a jittery rhythm.

He decided to go down to the kitchen for a sandwich, try to ground himself with the flavors of earth.

When he came to the kitchen door, Lana was standing in the center of the room, in nothing but her golden skin.

Toby awoke in the dark, Lana's perfect shoulder turned to him. As always, he could feel the power of their lovemaking winding down inside him. His arms and legs were sore.

He felt vaguely uneasy, but even more exhausted. A bolt of lightning flashed outside the window, blinding him for a moment while illuminating nothing. Shifting, he eventually settled back into unconsciousness.

Lana slept on.

She rose when dawn was still an hour away. From the closet, she drew a dress of pale green, cloudy as the color of the lake beyond the windows. It wrapped the curves of her breasts and backside in soft folds that whispered as she moved, turning her steps into half-heard endearments. She added white cotton gloves and blood-red sandals, lifting a straw tote bag from the closet shelf too. In the mirror, she smiled at herself.

Her shoes clicked faintly as she stepped across the room to the bed. Bending down, she murmured into Toby's ear.

"The knowledge of the flesh, unknown. The memory of night, undone. The triumph of the heart, unwound. No taste remains, no sight, no sound. Only man, forever bound."

Her dark curls twined off her shoulder and onto his, tenuously connecting their skin. A blue glow shone briefly all around Toby, then contracted, pulling itself up his body to the shoulder, to the very spot that her hair touched. The blue coiled up her curls and sank into her skin, which glowed with a renewed radiance.

She left the room and crossed the hall to the front door, then opened it and stepped outside onto the cool, dark sand.

The house faced the sea, which was still dim grey in the predawn light. A wind came off the waves, carrying the scent of salt and seaweed into her nose. She inhaled deeply, smiling, and walked down the stone path leading along the shore and over low dunes. As she walked, the sun slowly began to ascend. She passed tangled and broken jumbles of rotting wood, some still bearing figureheads that gazed emptily at the dunes. A name painted on one wreck caught the light as she turned down a curve in the path: *Swift*.

The path spread out into a flat space among the dunes that held a tall gray house. It was a perfect twin to the one where she had left Toby asleep.

She curled her lips into a smile, and opened the front door.

A bare-chested man, haggard, with graying hair and weathered cheeks, turned to face her. His skin swarmed with tattoos: two swallows in flight, a pair of dice, a cross. An inked rope coiled around his left wrist. "Ana," he whispered, reaching a hand toward her. Light bloomed in his eyes, a light vaguely tinged with blue.

She closed the door behind her with one curved hip.

>

Wiseacres
Jennifer Morales

THE WOMAN STANDS IN A YELLOW SUNDRESS AND sandals, snow circling her blue ankles. It's January in Milwaukee, Wisconsin, and she's out on the street half-naked. She's not one of the beggars that Dan's father, Buck, had told him to expect. She's not asking for money.

"Put a little bit of change in your front pocket," Buck had said as Dan was leaving home. "You got three days in town for the expo. Shake a little loose every day, but no more than a couple, like, five bucks total. Got it?"

In Buck's eyes he saw doubt.

"A dollar or two a day, no more. Don't be soft, Danny."

Dan's whole, miserable job at the building trades expo was handing out little keychains promoting their family business—Johansen Ladder Incorporated—and answering questions about bulk order discounts. He couldn't understand how his dad always came home from the expo all fired up. The chaos and noise of the vendor hall wiped Dan out and emptied his head of sense. Each morning, he left the convention center for a smoke and gave up a five to the first raggedy man who looked like he really needed it.

But the woman in the sundress isn't asking for money. She doesn't shiver or give any other sign of being cold as she goes through her routine: Wait for someone to approach. Lean in to say something to them. Wait. Give—or don't give—a flower from the battered, 5-gallon spackle bucket that hangs from her wrist.

It's Wednesday, the middle day of the expo. Dan's standing there smoking, trying to guess whether the next person will get a flower. He gets it wrong three times in a row—the first guy got a flower and Dan totally figured he wouldn't, then the old lady comes up and Dan thinks, *she's definitely getting a flower*, but she doesn't, and so on. Dan gives up and turns to watch the buses go hissing through the slush on Wisconsin Avenue. He knows she's got to be nuts, but eventually his curiosity gets the better of him. He grinds out his butt and strides over there, hitching up his new jeans as he goes.

She looks to be in her early 20s, young as his little sister. Her short hair is the color of coffee, and it gleams, concentrating the weak rays of winter sun.

"Cold enough for ya?" Dan says, though he knows the question is stupid. Her bare white arms are speck-led with gooseflesh.

She studies him with eyes the color of corn in early June. "Of course it's cold. But tell me this: What brings you joy?"

Her face is steady, seamless, giving no signal to him that this is some kind of joke. Her eyes have more depth to them than Dan would have guessed. Up close, the pale green goes mossy.

Her insistent gaze reminds him of the look his fifth-grade teacher, Mrs. Halvorsen, always gave him, one that said, *I bet you can figure this out on your own.* Back then, he just wanted Mrs. Halvorsen to tell him the right answer. She knew it already, so what was the point in risking being wrong?

"I said, 'What brings you joy?'" The woman is holding a purple carnation out just beyond Dan's reach.

His hand twitches in his pocket and he imagines himself grabbing the flower. He doesn't understand what she is asking him. He's heard of these people, street artists. There aren't any of them back home.

"Joy?" Dan hears himself say, puzzled, his teeth catching on the *J* as if he only recently learned English. He shakes his head, rousing himself out of her spell. "What's joy?"

Her hand lowers, dropping the purple flower back into the bucket. She looks away, toward the next supplicant, a weather-beaten man in a ripped jacket.

"I'll tell you all about joy, sweetheart," the man says. "I can tell you some stories for damn sure."

Dan goes back inside. He hands out ladder key-chains. He answers questions about volume discounts, about small business certification for municipal procurement. Later that night, he goes out for dinner at the 5 O'Clock Steakhouse with a sealants vendor and a guy from the carpenters' union. He tries three different kinds of whiskey.

Wiseacres. Dan's father warned him he'd meet a lot of them in the city.

"These hoity-toity types who think they know everything. Who think they're funny about it, too. Think they're getting one over on ya."

That woman must think she's funny. Out in the slush, asking people about joy. Does she think she's some kind of expert?

He looks for her the next day. Every smoke break— six of them—he strides the circumference of the convention center, two city blocks squared. His calves ache from the walking, the wet cold stiffening his jeans. But she's not there.

He tried asking people, back home.

At the Legion, catching the Packers game with his friend Tom, Dan asked him. "What brings you joy, man?" His throat caught on the question. It had taken him until halftime to get up the nerve.

Tom tipped his shaggy head back to pour in the last of the basket of pretzels. "It would give me some goddamn joy if they put Aaron Rodgers back in right now. If they kept their defense up, he wouldn't even be out with his goddamn collar bone broke in half."

Dan looked at the screen across the bar—one of eight in the small room, all tuned to the game. The Pack was down by 11. Would seeing Rodgers run out to the field right now really bring Tom joy?

"No, *joy*, man."

Tom looked at him out of the corner of his eye and then back to the screen. He hunched his shoulders. "What's that?"

Dan couldn't say. On the way home, he hit Walmart to look it up in a dictionary.

The emotion of great delight or happiness caused by something exceptionally good or satisfying; keen pleasure; elation.

Just to be sure, he looked up "keen"—*finely sharpened, as an edge; so shaped as to cut or pierce substances readily*—and "elation"—*a feeling or state of great joy or pride; exultant gladness; high spirits.*

High spirits or pleasure, sharp as a knife edge. When was the last time Dan felt that? Or the first? Where did Dan have room for that in the trailer he shared with his dad?

They had a real house once, before his mom got sick, a sturdy old brick one with the original oak woodwork and a stained-glass window in the front. On a sunny day it felt like living in a church. As a kid, Dan liked to lie in the planes of color, washing his hands in blue, orange, red. If he lay there long enough, the colors would travel the length of his body, a kaleidoscope transforming him a hair, an inch of denim, at a time.

When his mom got diagnosed, his dad struggled mightily to keep them all in health insurance. But the insurance company came up with some excuse to jack up the company's coverage, and they all lost it—Mom, Dad, Dan, his sister away at college, the five hired guys in the shop. They just didn't want to pay for her care.

Buck emptied their savings, and Dan took a second job. Even with all that, they had to sell the house and downsize to the trailer. Dan knew that's what finally killed her: knowing she was leaving them both broke and exhausted and, at the end, alone together in that cramped and humbling space. He saw it in her eyes.

Not that Dan thought he was better than anybody else here, although their trailer was the nicest one in the park. Buck wanted his wife to have some comforts, some beauty still. He had some Amish build a wrap-around porch and hung a glider swing to look out on the valley. At the foot of the porch he planted a fat row of pink roses.

"Dad, do you ever think about joy?" Dan asked, a couple weeks after the expo. He dreamed the night before of the green-eyed woman, her flowers.

"Your mother? Of course, you idiot. I was married to her for thirty years. What do you think?"

In all his musing on the word, it never clicked that Joy was his mom's name. Joy Ellen Johansen, born Joy Ellen Wilder. Of course, Dan always called her "Mom."

"Right. Besides that, though. I mean, the feeling joy."

"Damned if I know," Buck said. "She used to try to tell me that in low times I should look to her, that she would always be my joy." He shifted in his recliner, lifting up one buttock as if it hurt. It must hurt, Dan thought, him sitting there all day recovering from his heart attack while he knew things were going to shit at the shop.

His mom had held their lives together, at home and work, with threads invisible as a spider web. She was the connector. Dan recalled the mysterious trace of her hands as she taught him to tie his shoes, his eyes straining to capture each movement so that he could replay them in his head and emerge one day from his room, triumphant, his shoes tied.

"And your joy since—since Mom passed away?"

Buck grimaced, like Dan had released a bad smell into the room. After a minute he waved his son away, "Ah, forget about that."

From the shop office Dan watched the guys working the line, gluing yellow plastic caps on the feet of Johansen's cheapest model. Under their heavy filter masks—the ones that left red lines on their sweaty faces when they pulled them off at lunch—did any of them feel the sharp knife edge of joy? Sure, they joked around with each other in the breakroom—Dan used to be part of those jokes—but it was never anything deep. Now he couldn't even remember what was so funny.

Without his dad in the office, Dan had more to do but less attention for any of it. Lori, the admin, had to remind him before she left at 4:15 each day of something he forgot, some OSHA report, some paperwork Buck would need for the audit come spring.

The rough-paneled walls made the narrow, rectangular room feel smaller than it was. There remained an empty desk where Joy used to sit and smoke and type up the reports on the computer. The place still smelled like her Virginia Slims. Nobody was allowed to smoke in the office anymore.

He knew his dad expected him to take over the business when he retired—still a good ten or fifteen years off, Dan hoped—and he knew he should be grateful for it. But these weeks in charge while Buck recuperated left him agitated. Maybe he didn't want his dad's life, his business. Sometimes, after Lori and everyone had left, he felt like setting the place on fire.

Dan made up a reason to go back to the city every couple of months after the expo: His buddy won tickets from Rock 97.5 to a concert at The Riverside. He was going to a Brewers game with a high school friend who was working in Milwaukee now. There was a blowout sale at a sporting goods store in the burbs, and he was in the market for a new hunting rifle.

He enjoyed the challenge of coming up with new and semi-plausible excuses. Sometimes he would actually do the things he said he was going to do— go to the game, buy the rifle—and it seemed like maybe he was becoming someone else in those transactions, someone more interesting.

His girlfriend, Mickey, got suspicious of his sudden interest in visiting the city. "Why're you going there so much? And why can't I ever come along? You got another girl?"

To calm her, he took Mickey with him once. They toured the Harley Davidson Museum, played blackjack at Potawatomi, and strolled along the lake.

She watched him watch the streets.

"Who are you looking for?" Mickey asked, exasperation in her blue eyes. They were drinking bloodies and eating overpriced eggs at some industrial place in the Third Ward that the guy at the desk of their hotel said was good. In fact, the portions were small and everything was covered in cilantro.

"Nobody in particular. Just people watching, I guess. That's what you do when you come to a place like this, right?"

"I guess." She paused in salting her eggs to study him. "You've just been, I don't know, distracted a lot lately."

"Do you ever feel joy, Mick?"

It was coming on the anniversary of the day they met—three years ago, at a mutual friend's birthday cookout. Soon after that, Dan's mom got sick. Mickey had stood by him through her illness and death. He was thankful for that kindness, but had they shared any moments that counted as joy? He couldn't say.

"You're getting weird." She flicked a piece of cilantro onto the edge of her plate, then swabbed it off with her napkin. "And I don't like weird."

"I'm serious." He tried to laugh off her irritation. "Come on, Mick, just answer: When was the last time you felt joy?"

"Joy? You mean, like, happiness?"

"It's different than that. Happiness is like a long-term thing. Joy is . . ." He tried to think of an example she might relate to. "Like, when you're a kid and you and your friends rake together this huge pile of leaves and you jump into it. That feeling."

"I never liked that feeling. The leaves get down your shirt and there's ants and spiders and—no." She shuddered and scratched her back, as if something was crawling there.

"Well, something else then. I don't know—sledding. That feeling when you go over the edge of the hill and you can't stop and it's like you're flying?"

"Doesn't anything grownups do count as joy?"

"Grownups sled." He shrugged. "Maybe we should get a toboggan this winter. Or some tubes."

"Maybe we should get married. People always look happy on their wedding day." She squeezed his hand, but the smirk on her face confirmed that the suggestion was sarcastic.

Her sarcasm wounded him. The thought of proposing had crossed his mind once or twice. He loved her, loved the way she made him feel—desired, useful, steady—but it never seemed like the right moment. Now he wondered if his hesitation was rooted in something deeper than that.

"I'm not talking about happy, Mick. Joyful. Joy isn't happiness." He thought back to the dictionary definition. "It's sharp, quick. Something so good it cuts you open."

"I don't want to be cut open." She tossed her napkin on the table and crossed her arms over her chest. "You know, I don't understand anything that's going on right now."

On his next trip, Dan traveled alone, telling Mickey

that he had to go to the city for business. She didn't seem surprised. Since their weekend in Milwaukee, something between them had shifted.

Speeding down I-94, he loved the moment when the downtown suddenly revealed itself, each towering building full of people living lives so different from his. He craved the hours of anonymity in the city. Walking along the lakefront, admiring the tree-covered bluffs and the clean-swept beaches, the silvered apartment windows catching the sun, he was no one anybody recognized. Somehow this made him feel more himself.

That Friday evening, he wandered through the desolate mall on Wisconsin Avenue. At a tourist information kiosk, he picked up a brochure for Gallery Night. Forty galleries would be holding open houses in the neighborhoods surrounding downtown. The skin on his forearms prickled. Of course the green-eyed woman would be there, somewhere, among the other artists.

He had dinner at a café near his motel. While he ate his hamburger, he pored over the brochure, reading the descriptions of the art on display and circling the spaces with the most promise. Two locations said they were featuring performance art, one in the Third Ward and one in Walker's Point. He planned to start with those. Performance art was what the woman was doing, right?

He climbed to the first gallery, up a blinding, fluorescent-lit staircase lined in mosaics of broken glass, and found himself among a hundred people in a space built for fifty at most. More mosaics hung on the walls, all of them composed of clear glass and mirror. A disco ball suspended from the ceiling spun the room's white light into a slow, nauseating swirl.

"Glass of wine?" A woman dressed all in cream passed him a plastic cup. "Is this your first time at Art Den?"

Dan nodded.

"Well, welcome." The woman's huge teeth dominated her smile. "This is my gallery."

"Thanks." Dan didn't generally drink wine, but he downed the yellow liquid in two gulps. He wished it was beer.

"The mosaics are by Hyun-Ok Kowalski. She's a genius. The light. The refraction. Don't you think?" The toothy woman looked Dan up and down. She swept her satiny gray hair from her face, rattling an armful of acrylic bracelets. She was dressed to match the room. "You're from out of town, aren't you?"

"Viroqua."

"Oh, now that's a ways. Farm country. I initially read the Carhartt jacket and plaid shirt as ironic. Guess not." She snapped her fingers, as if striking out.

"This is just what I wear." He crushed the empty plastic cup in his hands. "I'm not trying to make a statement or anything like that."

"Let me tell you something." She grabbed his elbow and pulled him closer like she was going to let him in on a secret. "Everyone, darling—absolutely everyone—is trying to make a statement."

"I don't think so. I'm not." He thought of the

street artist and her flowers. "And I met this woman once who only asked a question. She would just stand on the street and ask people, 'What brings you joy?' She wasn't making a statement. Just asking a question."

"Are you talking about Aurora?" She furrowed her brow. "Darling, you make my very point. Aurora asking people that same question over and over, knowing that so many will fail to answer it, *is* a statement. It's art." Dan could hear the disapproval of him, his farm-country jacket—worn for real dirty work, not for show—in the way she bit down on the word "art."

"And what's the statement she—Aurora—is trying to make?" Discovering the woman's name gave him a flush of unexpected power. Certainly he would find her now, knowing her name.

"That people will fail. That they can't name a single thing that brings them joy. I thought I saw her on the bill tonight at Protean." The woman rolled her eyes. "I can't believe she's still doing that same shtick. Please."

"I guess I'm heading over to Protean, then." Dan had thought it was pronounced "protein." He handed the gallery owner his mangled wine cup.

"Well, tell Aurora I say hi." She was looking over his shoulder. Her face brightened, and Dan turned to see a well-dressed couple step over the threshold into the crowded room. "You'll have to excuse me," she said, squeezing his arm. "Because what brings me real joy is drunk art patrons with money in their pockets." The toothy woman moved away, slipping between the bodies like a shark through seaweed. "Edgar! Marcy!

I am absolutely ecstatic to see you here."

Protean was the gallery in Walker's Point that he
had circled in the brochure, the other one with perfor-
mances that night. It seemed like some kind of sign
to him that, all on his own, he had narrowed the list
down to two possibilities and he had found her. As
he drove the couple of miles, his GPS shepherding
him through the murky streets, he wondered what it
would be like to see her again. In his mind Aurora had
become larger than life, a riddling angel with some
essential knowledge he could gain if only he could
follow her instruction. He had been following it, questioning himself and those around him, and he felt a
door opening as a result. Where it led, he didn't yet
know, but it was opening. He shivered in his jacket,
although the early September air was warm.

In contrast with the Art Den's blaring whiteness,
Protean's raw space was dim. The two rooms off
to the right of the main gallery flickered with video
displays. The gallery to the left featured a series of
paintings illuminated by spotlights, leaving the rest
of the room in shadow. The main gallery, a high-
ceilinged room with exposed pipes gurgling overhead,
was ringed by six small stages.

On five of the stages, a single light highlighted a
chair or a prop of some kind, the artist either gone
already or yet to arrive. On the stage in the far corner,
a groaning man lifted something dark and boxy above
his head. Dan wedged himself into the crowd of
twenty or so watching him pick up an ancient cathode

ray-type TV set, hoist it above his head and grunt, then set it slowly down again. The TV was plugged in, tuned to static. The man's sweat dripped onto the set each time he placed it at his feet and his movements grew slower with every lift, the grunting resolving into a growl.

Dan turned to the rapt girl next to him. She seemed to be in her late teens and wore a brown leather vest over a lime green tank top and a purple-sequined ballerina skirt.

"What's this about?" he asked. Dressed like that, she couldn't possibly make him feel stupid for not getting it.

Without turning her head, she said, "I think maybe it's a commentary on the influence of media? The way our minds are so full of it all the time? Hold on a sec." She pulled her phone from her vest pocket and snapped a picture of the sweating man in all-out weightlifter grimace. "Crystal's going to love this." She pressed a few buttons, then dropped the phone back into her pocket.

"Did Aurora perform yet?"

The girl shook her head. "I don't think so. This is the first performance, I think. Who's Aurora? What does she do?"

"She's—well, I don't know. You'll just have to see it, I guess." Dan began moving away, suddenly wanting to keep the power of Aurora's art to himself. "Good to talk to you."

He wandered into one of the video galleries, where a black-and-white film in the style of a 1960s home movie played against the wall: a man and a woman in hippie clothes packing and unpacking a picnic basket in constant loop. The moment the woman placed the last Thermos in the basket, the film reversed and she was taking it out again. His mom was never a hippie, but she used to sigh sometimes that life was like this: the hamper refilling with laundry just soon as she had emptied it.

As his eyes adjusted to the shadows and the flickering video, he began to make out the faces in the room.

He sees her then. Aurora is leaned up against the wall to his right, arms crossed over her chest. This time she's dressed for the season, in a tweed skirt and tights, a light sweater with rhinestone buttons.

In the other room, the TV lifter's animal growl has become a roar that breaks through the silence of the picnic video.

Dan crosses the room and says, "Do you think that guy's OK?" He can't believe he's face to face with her again, after all these months.

Aurora shrugs. "I saw him warming up. He always stops before he breaks anything."

"Good. That's a relief." Dan forgets what he's relieved about before his mouth is even closed. He can only stare. In this light her eyes look gray.

"Do we know each other?"

"Not really. We met once. In January, outside the convention center downtown. You didn't give me a flower."

She laughs, then looks around the room. A couple of the video-watchers turn in their direction.

"Then you must not have deserved one." Her laugh is taunting.

"I do now."

"What?"

"Deserve one. A flower. I know what brings me joy."

She pats the small pockets of her skirt. "Fresh out, I'm afraid."

"I don't need the flower. I just wanted to tell you. And ask you something."

A husky man in a corduroy coat shushes them and Aurora jerks her head toward the door. Dan follows her back into the main gallery.

"What do you want to know?" Aurora checks her watch, a thin, silver band. "I'm on in ten minutes."

Dan hopes the smile on his face is as he feels it—inviting, not smug—but he can't help feeling pleased with himself. "I want to know, what brings you joy?"

She laughs out loud now, her head thrown back, her long arms sweeping toward the ceiling and crashing down onto her thighs. "All this time, no one's bothered to ask me that."

"Really?" Dan feels victorious. He's done something no one else has.

Her mouth falls open. "You know I'm kidding, right? Even the kid who cashiers at Walgreens asks me *what brings you joy* every time I go in there to buy tampons."

He doesn't want Aurora to see the disappointment in his face, so he turns toward the TV man's stage. A member of the audience has climbed up to help him lift, another squatting on the floor to spot him on the release. What do they think they're accomplishing, extending this guy's routine?

"I'm sorry. I'm being a smartass." Aurora pats Dan's shoulder. "Tell me your answer. What brings you joy?"

He shrugs off the weight of her hand, her gaze. "No, I don't think I'll tell you after all."

"I said I was sorry." A darkness crosses her face and she pulls on the sleeves of her sweater. "I'm on in a minute. I should go get ready."

"You don't know, do you?"

"What?"

"What brings you joy."

He makes record time on the trip home. As he speeds along the midnight landscape, he imagines that there must be someone out there worth telling.

➤

Paris in Texas
Tisha Marie Reichle-Aguilera

ISABEL GRIPPED THE DOORKNOB TIGHTLY, STEPPED out the back door and onto the back step. The tall old salt cedar trees cast wide shadows that didn't quite reach her until the sun fell behind Coyote Mountain.

Yoli reached out to hold Isabel's hand, distracted for a moment by two neighbors from across the circle.

"Hello there!"

"*Como sientes?*"

Yoli waved and whispered, "They are loud when they—you know."

"Do I look like I care about their sex life?" Isabel scowled. "I almost died. The doctor said I lost a lot of blood in there." But she didn't look at Yoli, hid how grateful she felt for this loss. She didn't need two more children. Five at home was enough. She squinted into the sun, tried to conjure the faces of her two oldest sons, the baby she'd left behind and the one who'd been stolen from her. She hoped Jaime had learned a lot from Miss Julie, gone to college like her son had. David would be in high school now, probably had a new mother, more siblings. Probably didn't know she existed.

Isabel dropped a yellow cushion onto the concrete and sat near her new plants. She stared at them, knew they would listen to her woes. "Even though the twins were dead, I still had to give birth as if they were alive." Isabel felt a tug in her abdomen, an ache between her legs, and relief in her voice. "*Mi Viejo*, he couldn't stop crying."

Yoli took the last drag of her cigarette, eyebrows raised. "You sure you're okay to be out here? I can do it by myself." She reached down for the lantana. "If Caro was here, you wouldn't even need me. You heard from her?"

Isabel shook her head and swallowed the lump in her throat. It had been several months since her second daughter, Carolina, had left home with the carnival worker. Every morning Isabel's husband, Armando, lit a candle and prayed for her safety. Every night, the oldest, Julia, cried herself to sleep. Isabel listened for Caro's return, regretted letting her go so easily, and hoped she'd been wrong about her daughter's new life.

"Lucky flame," Isabel read from the plastic tag. She'd ordered the bright orange and yellow flowers before she went to the hospital. Yoli'd been sprinkling them with water every other evening while Isabel was in bed last week. If she didn't plant them today, they could die. And she didn't trust Yoli to do it right. "We're going to give you a new home, *preciosas*," she whispered into the pungent leaves.

Yoli snorted at Isabel's *cariños*. She'd never understood how to love her plants.

"*Aquí?*" she asked, dangling the roots over the damp earth.

"*Allá.*" Isabel pointed a little more left with her big toe, its tip touched the cool soil.

Yoli dug more holes for the salvia.

"These two didn't help at all. The other kids wanted to escape. All four girls and even Junior's giant head— *no problema*. But these two wanted to live inside me forever. *Ay no!* At least they were small." Jaime had been small too. Really small. Miss Julie said Isabel was lucky he could breathe on his own when he was born. Isabel took a cigarette from Yoli's pack and puffed gently. "It has been too long since I enjoyed this."

Yoli took it from her, inhaled deeply, and held in her smoke a little. "What's next?"

"My summer jewel." Isabel loosened the long velvety stems from their plastic shell. "Put these in the back row." She imagined the bright red blooms scattered across the dull off-white stucco building. "*Cuidado,*" Isabel said before taking another short puff. "They're fragile."

"Are they even gonna live through summer? It's supposed to be hotter than ever."

"It's always hotter than ever here." Isabel closed her eyes and wished for a cool breeze, a gust of wind that didn't reek of chemicals or manure. "I had to name them, you know. *Mi Viejo* tried to be strong, held my hand while the priest gave Joseph and Magdalena their sacraments."

"He said you fainted." Yoli took a drag from the cigarette, left it between her lips and reached for the last salvia plant. "He said the nurse thought you were having another baby."

"*Por tonta.* She probably never had a baby. How would she know?" Isabel lowered her voice. "They took everything out. Said it wasn't gonna work right anymore. Might as well." She grabbed her belly flesh with both hands. "Maybe this *panza* will finally go away." She reached up for another puff, but Yoli had finished the cigarette with one long drag. "At least I can't get pregnant anymore. Thank God." Isabel cursed herself when she saw Yoli's lingering sadness.

When Isabel and Armando had first moved from Central California to this Imperial Valley neighborhood with the two older girls, Yoli was all *celosa.* "You'll never be alone," she'd said. Her sadness sat in the heat.

When Isabel had repeated what Yoli'd said, "I'll never be alone," it was with dread. This wasn't the life she'd imagined when she was younger. She wanted to travel but not to work fields in another dusty town. She had dreamed about places she'd only seen on the globe at school, wanted to learn new languages too.

"Closer to the edge." Isabel pointed again with her other foot so Yoli didn't put the last plants too close to the rest. The portulaca needed space to grow wide. Its thick needle leaves would fill the corner of the bed, a barrier protecting the more delicate blooms.

No one protected Isabel like that. Her delicate was gone when she had her first son at fourteen. Nine kids later, she could finally stop. Maybe be free. But it was too late for dreams. She only knew Spanish and English and hadn't made a world wish in years.

"Should I water them all now?" Yoli stood, dusted the grains of soil off her knees, and twisted her back.

The foulness of her sweat made Isabel's eyes water. She coughed. "Gracias, Yoli. I can manage the hose." But first she lengthened her legs and put both feet flat on the earth. She closed her eyes and tilted her face toward the setting sun. "Palermo," she said.

"*Qué?*"

"Barcelona."

"What?"

"Casablanca." Isabel opened her eyes wide, and Yoli's crotch was too close to her face. She leaned back and reached both hands up.

Yoli helped her stand.

"That's all I can remember." Isabel imagined her elementary classroom. Kids had screamed and chased each other with sticky hands. Someone's milk had gone sour. She had spun the blue/brown metal ball, watched it with her head tilted sideways so the words were straight. She had ignored the chaos around her and waited for the globe to slow before she placed a fingertip on its bumpy surface, stopped the spinning with her destination choice. "Of all the places I wanted to visit, I can only remember those three names." Names in Spanish. The others she couldn't really pronounce. But she'd touched the raised black letters and spelled them to the smart kids nearby. A nice boy with green eyes and freckled nose had said the names for her. Isabel had repeated what she'd heard and smiled with gratitude. But that was all lost now.

"Who'd you be visiting?" Yoli asked and sat on Isabel's yellow cushion. "Your family?"

"My family was swallowed by Texas. When I was a kid, I just wanted to go." Isabel turned her back to Yoli and moved the trickle of water slowly over her plants. Wet and shiny and new. "*Mira que bonitas*," she said to them. "In a few weeks, your beautiful blooms will make all the neighbors jealous."

"Nobody just goes like that, Chavela." Yoli got another cigarette.

"People do."

"Not our people." Yoli took a few short puffs. "What about Paris?"

"No!" Isabel's voice is sharp, louder than she expected. So loud it hurt her gut and echoed across the circle. "No," she repeated more quietly. "Never Paris."

"Because you don't know French?"

"Because there's a Paris in Texas. We drove through there once." That memory singed the innocence of her schoolgirl dreams. She closed her eyes and tried to keep her hot, dusty past from returning. She and Julia had left Texas with a man who promised California would be different. He was no different from her first husband. She held her lower abdomen, still pained from its recent loss. "I almost lost Carolina," she whispered. The pop-pop of a passing car made her gasp and open her eyes wide.

"We could learn French," Yoli said, oblivious to Isabel's pain. "Maybe buy those tapes."

"You could do that." Isabel let the cool water splash speckles of soil onto her ankles.

Yoli passed the cigarette to Isabel. A crop duster flew over them, had dumped its toxins in a nearby field. They traded the cigarette back and forth until it was done.

"If you don't need me anymore," Yoli said, "I'm going home now. Maybe tomorrow we'll travel." Yoli flip-flopped on the asphalt, shuffled slowly back across the circle.

Isabel wiggled her toes in the edge of the mud, drizzled the cool water over them, and whispered to her plants, "Palermo, Barcelona, Casablanca."

The Stone Frog

Jeanette Weaskus

HE WAR CHIEF AWOKE FROM A DREAM OF SEVERAL hundred dogs flying through the air at great speed so that very morning went to see the holy man to decipher the meaning of this dream. The trip took the better part of a day, and the chief, not wanting to be alone, took his son and his nephew along for company. The cousins were very much like twins, and so where one went, the other was also to be found. Their horseback ride went along pleasantly enough with plenty of laughter amongst the three, horseracing to certain points along the way, and stopping for lunch halfway through the trip. They arrived where the holy man lived in time for the evening meal. Now it was in those old Indian days that all the animals who had thus angered Coyote and got turned to stone for their transgressions used to still be able to come alive at night, so children were not allowed outside after dark lest one of those stone animals take them away.

Near the holy man's camp was Miss Frog, who had been turned to stone when she mistreated her husband Badger, Coyote's best friend. The children who lived in the camp were not allowed to play near Miss Frog, but the next day they took the war chief's boys over to see the great rock. The eldest boy jumped atop Miss Frog and straddled her like a horse. Her back was covered in moss still wet from the morning dew, causing him to slide down. He clutched at her head to keep from slipping off and in doing so covered up her eyes with his hands. She thought it was nighttime and immediately came to life, jumping towards the riverbank. The boy let out a war whoop at the novel experience of riding a giant stone frog. His cousin, not wanting t him to have all the fun, also jumped on the frog.

The frog sped along at terrific speed for it was large in size and very strong from being made of basalt. They flew through the air, laughing and hanging onto her back with all their strength. At last they stopped at a large buffalo hide tipi which Miss Frog told them was Coyote's lodge. She asked them to go inside and look at all of Coyote's treasures for a beaded purse that once belonged to her great-grandmother frog. The boys went inside and saw that the tipi had a great many painted rawhide parfleches containing war shirts made in the designs of all the surrounding Indian tribes. The boys looked through them until each found a good Nez Perce style shirt to wear. Coyote's weapon collection was an almost endless array of war clubs, bows, arrows, knives, and spears. The boys took a club and some flints before proceeding on to a collection of beaded items including bags, gloves, saddles, moccasins, and knife sheaths. They found a beaded bag with an image of two frogs, which they took. After seeing all the marvels of Coyote's lodge, the boys emerged and jumped back onto Miss Frog, covering her eyes so that she could move once again.

"Take us back to the holy man's camp," said the war chief's son, and that is where she leapt. The taller boy kept her eyes covered and told her they had her bag. This they gave to her and both threw their arms around her neck and thanked her for the wonderful ride to Coyote's lodge. When she put her beaded bag into her pocket, Miss Frog also took out two opals to reward them for returning her bag that had been taken by Coyote. The opals were a great treasure as the very old ones could render their owner invisible. The boy removed his hands from her eyes and she returned to sleep for the day. Just as the children were returning to camp for the mid-day meal, the war chief came upon his boys and they began the ride home.

Although there were a great many kinds of treasures in Coyote's lodge, the boys only took weaponry for themselves. Through the years, they practiced with the clubs, made arrows for the flints and became accomplished marksmen. With the magic of these war items taken from Coyote's lodge that day, these two boys grew into the greatest warriors of the Nez Perce Tribe. History knows the eldest of the boys who rode Miss Frog as Chief Joseph and his cousin as Ollocut, the war chiefs who led the Nez Perce people away from General Howard during what has become known as The Nez Perce War of 1877.

⟍

<

Let Kari Float Down
Erika T. Wurth

DRIVE TO THE GROCERY STORE FOR SOME BUTTER, AND on the way I remember not to think about her. It's easy most days because I have made it so that she is under the surface, under the surface of me. Keeping her down in the dark, though it horrifies me to think of her that way, is the only way I can keep myself in the light, keep myself going, going to the grocery store for butter.

"Hey sweetie," my wife says when I come home, and kisses me while I live with Kari everywhere while she does it, her lips on mine. My kind, kind lips. So kind. So soft, Kari once said. It was one of her few compliments, and she was drunk. "Did you get the butter?" she asks, narrowing her eyes a little, and I nod, my head moving up and down with the swift motion of pushing Kari down. "Good," my wife says, and I smile, my lips soft, my finger at the fullest point of them, remembering. She seems preoccupied, or maybe she can feel me, feel my heart, where it's at, where it is not.

My wife is white, of course she is, like my mother, white and safe and from a background like mine. Though not like mine, because I am Indian, I am Ute, and Kari was like me, though not like me. Chickasaw and rough and poor and beautiful. And she did not love me. Or she did, but the way she did was like not loving me at all, or worse.

I sit down at the plain wooden table that my plain wooden wife wanted, and I pull out my phone so I can look at the news and shake my head and sit at the table for long enough to make her feel like I want to be in her presence, which I do not. I don't know if she feels the same way, and I don't want to know, because I am kind, and kind men don't think that way.

"Sold a house today," she says, straightening her pale white suit, her pale beige heels by the door, her feet bare. I tell her congratulations and shift in my seat. I am uncomfortable in the way I have been ever since I met her. It's why I married her, punishment for my heart. I was actually kind once, I remember, and it's not Kari's fault that I'm not kind now, though I am nice, the way my white neighbors are nice, the way they condescend to be nice to me. Though I can tell, they don't like it, they don't like me. The feeling is mutual, but Sheryl, my wife, wanted to live here, said it was a good neighborhood to raise children. I remember when she said it and shudder.

"Which one?" I ask nicely, but I don't care, because Kari wouldn't and she is living with me all day in the dark. Kari—drinking a Bud and laughing loud and sweet and like an Indian woman. Not polite like my wife, who is white, who loves this neighborhood, a good neighborhood to raise children.

Maybe my wife hates it like me. Maybe she is like me. Maybe she lives with someone else in the dark, in her heart, but I don't think so. She doesn't love me, at least I don't think so. That is a relief at least. Unlike other men, I have never tried to fool myself. That doesn't work with me. I've never told myself that I love her. I have told her, but only when I must, in a nice way, to be nice.

The thing about my wife is that she isn't smart, and she isn't beautiful, and I don't fault her for either of those things. She is a human being, and my unhappiness has nothing to do with her beyond that she is a reminder that Kari didn't love me. My wife likes cooking shows, and she still has her little brown teddy bear from when she was young. She is a human being. I am ridiculous, I cannot get over it, over Kari, though I leave her alone, because she asked me to. She is a human being, she deserves to move on with her life, though it hurts me and I Google her every day, looking for something, but there is nothing. She is not on social media. She wouldn't be. Kari would consider it a waste of time. I am on Facebook and Twitter and Instagram, and it says "Married" and it says "Architect" and it says "Highlands Ranch" and it has pictures of me at the beach, and at Disneyland, though we do not have children. My wife loves Disneyland, and we go every year and eat ice cream and go on the *It's a Small*

World ride while my wife's eyes fill with childlike wonder and I hate it because I know Kari would, because in all honesty I hate it, me, alone, myself. And I hate my wife, though I do not hate her, I hate myself, and I love Kari, and I can't get over it.

My wife leans against the granite counter and looks up from her phone. "How's the new project going?"

"Good. Bob is finally ready to take my suggestions."

"Good," she says. Everything is always good. She looks down at her phone again, her mouth pinching at something she sees, or thinks, her short, highlighted hair waving and covering her little, pale, freckled face. A face another man would've found endearing, and it is. I love her in a way because I am used to her, and she is a human being who deserves at least respect if not love, so there is a way in which I love her.

Denver is a booming city. It is rich. It is expensive, and I wonder where Kari lives in it every day. And by every day, I mean every minute. There is not a moment when I have relief so I have kept her in the dark, always with me. Sometimes I tell my wife I have to work late, and I drive around Colfax where I know the other Indians live, and I look for her, not to talk to her because she told me to go. That would be cruel and frankly unkind, and also she has the right to say no, I always loved that she did. I think if I could glimpse her I would feel . . . fulfilled. Like magic was back in my life, if only for a second. I could eat that second up, fill myself with that little glimmer of time, and live for it for a while. I wouldn't care what she looked like, though I have a feeling she is the same. She was not beautiful, she was magical, she had hair like a thousand brown-red fireworks, long, and in my hands, my face inside it, my eyes closed, I was whole.

My wife puts her phone down on the counter and sits next to me at the table. I put my phone down and look up at her and smile, and push Kari down further, as far as she can go without dying.

"Let's go out tonight," she says, smiling, like a child, her lips pulling up just a bit at the corners. I think if I loved her she would put her hand over mine and I would squeeze her hand and I would feel my heart move like an unborn child, one whose heart has just begun to beat, but she doesn't, and I never do. We only meet late at night three times a year, when I am half asleep, and I must have what most human beings must have, and so must she. And when it is over, we roll over, and we never kiss, only in front of others or when I first come home, briefly, to be nice.

"Sure. Where?" I ask and she smiles again, wider. There is something in her little light brown eyes.

We go out at least half of the days of the week because we have money. We are middle class, and we have no children, it's nice, we have money. Money for granite counter tops and an office to myself with all of the things my spiritual leader gave me when I was young, when I did that ceremony, when I thought I would have children with Kari and teach them our languages. But there is no one to do that with now. And I cannot keep those things in our bedroom. They would scare my wife, and frankly, it would make me sick, sick in my spirit, and I am already sick there. In all honesty, I hurt.

"Chinese?" I ask, because she loves Chinese and I am nice. And I don't hate it. It was the one food besides hamburgers and Mexican food Kari would eat. I always get what she ordered twenty years ago, Kung Pao Chicken, and I imagine I have her mouth while I eat it, closing my eyes and dreaming and knowing that I am sick but that this is the only way I can deal with the sickness. It is too big for my elders now, even if I still knew them, which I do not. Even if I still spoke parts of my language, which I do not. Those words live even further down in the dark than Kari does, where they are warm, where they are safe, safe from this life.

She claps her hands briefly and this time I smile, I am nice.

"I'll go get ready," she says, "unless . . . you don't want to go out?" She looks worried, strange, and I reassure her, and she walks up the stairs. I do not watch her. I look down at my phone. And then it comes, the surge that happens to me once a week, the thing I push down all the time rising up, and I do it. I put her name in the phone like it is magic and this time I will see something. But I don't. I thought I did years ago, something about court and charges, and it frightened me. I wanted to find out more so that I could find her by any means and save her, hold her, make her OK. But it disappeared, that small thing on the computer, when all I had was a computer, and no matter how I tried, I couldn't get it back. God, I could never get it back.

Sometimes I wish she would die or I would die so

that this could be over. When I think about my own death, I'm mainly indifferent though that makes me sad. It makes me sad mainly for my mother, who loved me so much, and in a way, sad for my father, who left when I was so young. He was Ute. He never called again. He drank. That wasn't a stereotype. That was real. I am thankful that is not part of my sickness. But my mother, she died a few years ago of cancer. She worried so much that I stopped drinking around her and it made her happy. I liked to make her happy. She was a good person. Not just nice, but good. My wife is like a pale imitation of my mother. My mother liked her, the way she never liked Kari, who could feel that. Kari was a reminder of our distance, one that would never close, a reminder of who I was, of who she wasn't, of my father, who my mother loved.

My wife and my mother would talk in the kitchen and share recipes like women do on television and they would laugh, small, polite laughter that wouldn't scare anyone, not like Kari's, which was wonderful. Which was Kari. I like to be scared.

But thinking of Kari's death is unbearable. It keeps me up at night. It fills my stomach like blood, like an ocean of pain. The only reason I wish for it is because then I would know what happened to her. Her absence is like a wide, great thing I live with, and am embarrassed because why can't I get over her? I'm not crazy. I don't love her so much I hate her. I just love her, and I can't not love her. It's not who I am.

She comes down the gray carpeted stairs, my wife, and she has put lipstick on, pale pink, and I know she is excited for this small, new adventure and I guess so am I. These things get us out of the house, and except for my office it is not a place I like, it is not my place. It is 2,500 square feet of box filled with things I don't care about.

At the restaurant she folds her napkin over her small, polite lap. She will order sesame chicken. She will not eat much of it. She is little, she is thin, she goes to the gym and almost never drinks. Sometimes a glass of white wine, that is all. I have never seen her drunk. I saw Kari drunk all the time, and she was beautiful because she drank for fun, not for pain, and never too much. Just enough to move into a place of heightened beauty, and she would push me a little, but like I said, I like to be scared.

"Are you OK?" my wife asks, and I say yes, and I suppose she believes me. Sometimes I'm not as good at not pushing it down. Right now I'm not good at pushing it down. I will order a drink. I will order another.

My wife cocks her head like she doesn't believe me, and I wonder.

"Just you two?" the waitress asks, and I nod. My wife expects me to. Kari would've gotten mad at me for doing anything on behalf of both of us. But my wife likes it. She looks down at the menu and so do I, as if either of us will order what we haven't ordered countless times before.

It's time to make polite conversation, something about the neighbors, and something about something that they are doing that is scandalous, that is bad, but not really. I thought she would be staring at her menu, or at her phone, or at her hands, or at other people, but she is staring at me. She never stares at me, the way I used to stare at Kari. I never stare at her, the way I used to stare at Kari. Kari would never stare at me, though sometimes I would catch her looking, a mix of pity and annoyance on her face. Though sometimes I wondered if I didn't see love, maybe just a little, though she never said it, not once, no matter how I wished she would. I tried not to say it to her too much. I knew she didn't want it, but I loved her and convinced myself she loved me. I was fifteen.

"Hi," I say and I try to sound friendly and confused.

"Hi," she says, her cheeks turning red. Like we'd just met. Like she had been caught staring at a stranger, which she had.

"Are you OK?" she asks again and my eyebrows come together, my thick, dark eyebrows that I have to pluck or they would never be in a perfect, white people, curved, line.

"I . . . you asked me that before," I answer.

"Oh, I'm, I'm sorry." She says I'm sorry a lot. Every day. To me. To people in line at the post office. To people in the street if her arm brushes their arm, to everyone, to everyone.

"Don't be sorry," I say, but I am. I'm sorry she is asking me if I am OK. "What's wrong?" I ask, and she turns away, smooths her thick, black napkin down on her lap.

"Nothing. Nothing," she says, and I feel relief. I

know I should push her, that's what a good husband does, but I don't because I'm not a good husband, I'm a nice one.

She begins talking about a woman at work who bullies her. I nod sympathetically until the waitress comes, a booster seat under her arm. She starts to put the booster down in the seat next to us and I stop her.

"We—we didn't ask for this," I say, and she stops, picks it up.

"No booster?" she asks. "No children?"

"No," I say, and the woman leaves.

My wife is silent. She's always silent when it comes to this, to children. I give her a minute to come back together, to get her head back where it has to be and yet she seems to need more time than usual and I wonder and I worry. I like to be nice.

"You were saying?" I prompt her. "About, you know, work?"

"Yesssssss," she says, drawing it out strangely, like a cartoon, like she has suddenly developed a neurological disorder, like she is going to have a breakdown and that is Kari. But not the kind of Kari I like. The kind that could bring all of this down. No matter how much I hate it, I live for it too, our lives together, the lies, the small things we do, they kept me from doing things like going to Colfax all the time, becoming one of those men you shake your head at, one of those men who can't take no for an answer, one of those men I hate.

"You said she didn't want to hear about your idea?"

"She didn't," my wife says, and I breathe a huge

sigh, one that takes my shoulders up, and then down.

"She—" my wife begins, but she is interrupted by our drinks, hers is wine, mine is scotch. I need it. I keep some in my office, and late at night, I drink it and go to the computer, hoping it is magic, hoping for her name.

I sip eagerly and my wife does the same and when I look back up, she is staring at me again, and I know this is over. She's going to do something that will ruin this thing that we have and there is nothing I can do to get out of it.

"Who is, I mean, I have to know. Who is Kari James?" she asks, the words like a dam bursting from her small, thin lips. I feel the air go out of me like she's punched me with her small, thin hand.

"How do you know that name?" The fact that she's said her name makes me sad, makes Kari's name so small. Her knowing feels like poison.

"I'm sorry, I'm sorry, I'm sorry, I just . . . ." Her lip begins to tremble, like it did when she found out we couldn't have children, and I know if she cries people will look and things are already very, very bad.

"It's OK," I say, "I'll tell you. It's no big deal. I'll tell you. I'm sorry you feel bad or weird. It's OK."

Her lip continues to tremble. I take a long sip of the scotch, and then I take the rest of it in my mouth. I signal the waitress, the waitress with the goddamn booster, for another. And maybe another. Just one more would get me through this night.

"She was a high school girlfriend, that's all," I say, and smile. It's true, I'm telling the truth.

"OK," she says, but she isn't done and I feel Kari

coming out of the darkness to laugh at me, to mock me, to ask why the fuck I can't get over her. Jesus, why.

"How do you know her name?" I ask, but shouldn't have. I feel sick, I want to drown.

"I went to your—computer. I—just needed to Google something and my phone was in the car and my computer was down and I needed . . . to know something. And when I went to Google her name came up."

"I looked her up. Curious," I say too fast, waiving the waitress down who took my drink order.

"Yes. Oh, of course. I do that. But—"

And I wait.

"For some reason I clicked on the history. You—you Google her all the time. It must be every day," her head is down. She's crying. She shouldn't be. She doesn't love me. That was the deal. There isn't love so what I'm doing is OK, it's mutual.

"I just—was curious."

I say nothing and I think she might move on, and let me push Kari back down into the dark, where she is safe.

"Every *day*, Sam!" she says, raising her voice. "It's embarrassing!"

Now I'm the one who is quiet because now we will both be living with Kari.

"I loved her once, you know," I say, taking another drink but the glass is empty. I close my eyes. Then, "Let's drop it. It's no big deal."

She's quiet, and our food comes, and my third scotch. I drink and I look at my wife, Sheryl, a human being who I had to think of as empty, and she smiles, her eyes lighting up, just a little, and then the woman with the booster seat comes again, and starts to put the booster in the seat again. Jesus she's really struggling to get it in there and at first I am speechless and then I am angry. So angry I almost yell. But I don't yell. I stop myself. Because there's nothing more dangerous than being brown in a restaurant full of white people, and being angry and brown and yelling in a restaurant full of white people.

We are both quiet now. I drink my scotch. I'm lucky they had given it to me. I hope that later I can get my wife to talk about work, about the house she sold, if I could just get her to talk about anything, something nice, she would let Kari float down, all the way back down home, in the place far under my heart.

My wife nibbles at her food like a tiny white rabbit, and I push my steak around like a moose, and I think about the booster seat and I think about the waitress and my anger, and as we eat I remembered going to the doctor right after I asked Sheryl to marry me.

Another waitress comes up, thank God not the one with the booster seat, and my wife tells the waitress that the food was very good, thanks, and that no she doesn't want another drink, thanks, and she smiles at me, and she opens her mouth and closes it.

I smile back, and swallow my meat. Things are going well. I remembered at the doctor's office, his clean white office, my tall brown body up on the large plastic bed, it was covered in paper. He was nice. It was an outpatient procedure. It was quick. It didn't really hurt. He cut those parts clean. Now, I look at my wife and I picture a meadow, one close to the mountains, so wide, so pure, green. Kari and I had gone camping once. I had felt something move there. And though it is sick, I feel happy, meat in my mouth, blood at my tongue. I can see Kari's face, her sharp brown eyes looking into me, her hair pouring down her neck like earth, my lips at her throat, which was shaking with laughter. I think about what I wanted. Children with Kari, their hair brown, thick, their tiny bodies sitting square during a sweat, their faces lit up at ceremony, their hands reaching for an eagle feather, theirs. I look over at my wife as if in a dream, thank God for the scotch, thank God for my sickness.

My wife's face begins to float and I think about how I will ask her to drive home, how I will hand her the keys and then I will sleep, and I will go to that place I keep under my heart, the place where Kari lives, my home, my true home. I blink slowly, dreaming, I am dreaming. When my wife and I weren't able to have children, I comforted her when she cried, which wasn't that much. But to have children with anyone except for Kari, no, no, no, that is wrong, it is sick. And I am already sick. I am already so far from home.

⟶

CONTRIBUTORS' NOTES

JINWOO CHONG is the author of the novel *Flux*. He received an MFA from Columbia University. His short stories have appeared in *The Southern Review*, *Chicago Quarterly Review*, and *Salamander*. He lives in New York.

I started 'The Lesser Light of Dying Stars' a month into the pandemic and was inspired by the firsthand-account feature writing that had started to pop up in some of the larger newspapers and magazines. I'm thinking specifically of 'How New Jersey's First Coronavirus Patient Survived,' in *The New York Times Magazine*, which chronicled the infection timeline of physician assistant James Cai in an extremely intimate and terrifying close third person (those looking for fiction in the same vein might try Alice McDermott's 'Post,' which appeared last year in *One Story*). This was the first story I'd written in a kind of 'global' voice, dipping in and out of various points of view as a fictional pandemic runs its course. It's tough for me to read back, to be honest. I think many are still healing from trauma. But what seems to have interested journalists about the pandemic has always been the aspect of personal humanity. It's been stunning to see the amount of moving, prescient storytelling that has come from our collective experience in this way.

RISË KEVALSHAR COLLINS is a writer living in Boise. She studies creative writing at Boise State University where she's also served on the editorial staff of *Idaho Review*. Risë earned an MSW at University of Houston, and wrote psychosocial assessments across Texas, Oregon, Washington State, and Idaho. (A joke, yet it's true.) She earned a BFA at Carnegie-Mellon University and was a member of the original Broadway production of *For Colored Girls Who Have Considered Suicide / When the Rainbow is Enuf* by Ntozake Shange. Risë performed solo—as an actor—at Carnegie Recital Hall. Risë's (first and only) play, *Incandescent Tones*, was produced off-Broadway and in repertory theatres. Her op eds have been featured in *Idaho Statesman*, *Boise Weekly*, and *Blue Review*. Risë was featured on the Idaho PBS online series *The 180*. Her nonfiction appears in *Michigan Quarterly Review* ('Shabda') and in *The Texas Review* ('Zaki: I Rise to Write the Story'); her fiction ('White Bird') appears in *North American Review*; her poetry appears in *The Indianapolis Review, Tupelo Quarterly, The Minnesota Review, and ANMLY*. Risë has been awarded a grant by The Alexa Rose Foundation.

'White Bird,' my fiction story, was first published in *North American Review*. The story was inspired by my time spent working and living alone in remote, rural, long-wintered, conservative, white, Christian, North

Idaho. The experience was augmented by my being a southern-born American woman of African ancestry for whom creativity, embrace of and contribution to people kind are among my commitments. I've traveled broadly. Within my homeland I've moved fifty-one times. There is a hunger in this land for love. There is an opening in this land for love. I write from and into this space. Natural beauty and equal justice are two of my 'triggering subjects.' Cities across the U.S. in general, and in North Idaho in particular, are among my 'triggering towns.'

Faculty in the MFA Creative Writing program at the Institute of American Indian Arts, **JAMIE FIGUEROA** is the author of the critically acclaimed novel, *Brother, Sister, Mother, Explorer*. Her writing has appeared in *McSweeney's*, *American Short Fiction*, *Agni*, *Elle*, and *Emergence Magazine*, among others. Boricua by way of Ohio, Jamie lives in northern New Mexico.

There were literally bunnies, just as described in the opening to 'Like None Other' in the yard where I was living at the time in Santa Fe. It was too good of a detail to pass up. The world is constantly trying to get our attention, offering itself up to us in detail after detail. It can be hard to receive given the chaos and clutter of our lives. Still, as writers, that's the invitation, it's part of the practice. I hold a deep inquiry around identity and being of mixed race/heritage. This along with ancestry and place drives my writing. Simultaneously, I bear witness to white women who are trying to understand their own context and how their response or non-response adds to the field of ignorance and fragility, or, to the field of awareness and justice. I write my characters through a BIPOC lens, similar to myself, as a way to honor and amplify underrepresented perspectives. In the tender complexity of the nuclear family, especially the mother/daughter bond, I wanted to explore a perspective I had yet to inhabit on the page—that of a white woman undergoing significant transformation both physical and symbolic—and anchor the story there. While I aimed to avoid sentimentality, the story is incredibly emotional, which surprised me as I wrote it and surprises me still when I read it to an audience.

LIBBY FLORES is a 2008 PEN Center USA Emerging Voices Fellow. Her writing has appeared in *The Kenyon Review*, *Gagosian Quarterly*, *American Short Fiction*, *Ploughshares*, *Post Road Magazine*, *Mc Sweeney's*, *Tin House / The Open Bar*, *The Guardian*, *Paper Darts*, and *The Los Angeles Review of Books*. She is the Associate Publisher at *BOMB* magazine. Libby holds an MFA in creative writing from Bennington College. She lives in Brooklyn, but will always be a Texan. She is represented by Sarah Bowlin at Aevitas Creative Management.

How the story came about: It was the first line. It almost always is for me. 'My life was a morsel at the time,' haunted me for a time, and once I wrote it down I saw an image of a guy who always stared at doorways wishing for his wife to appear. Longing is my Achilles' heel when it comes to characters; there is so much to learn when desire shows up. It is hard to resist the why and all the unfinished business in between.

←

JANE HAMMONS grew up on a farm in Roswell, New Mexico, and taught writing at UC Berkeley for thirty years before returning home to the Southwest to write and practice photography. Her writing appears in a number of magazines and anthologies: *Alaska Quarterly Review*, *Contrary Magazine*, *Hint Fiction* (Norton), *The Maternal Is Political* (Seal Press), *Selected Memories* (Hippocampus Press). Three of her photographs were included in *Taking It to the Streets: A Visual History of Protest and Demonstration in Austin*, an exhibition of the Austin History Center. She is a citizen of the Cherokee Nation of Oklahoma.

I wrote this story in the 1980s when I had just begun writing short fiction after mainly writing poetry for several years. Playing in its background is Springsteen's 'Nebraska' (1982) and the closing line he attributes to the murderer Charles Starkweather when asked why he killed: 'Well, sir, I guess there's just a meanness in this world.'

Toss in the election of Ronald Reagan (meanness personified). Mix a dose of dark humor to the landscape of my childhood, a rural area south of Roswell, New Mexico, and you have 'A Place Called Beautiful.'

It was about 10,000 words when I began submitting it in the '80s. With rejections, I often received useful critiques and revised. I also received not-useful critiques, that contained numerous admonitions in the form of *you can't* and *don't* statements, often about the opening paragraph, written in second person.

I could no more cut that paragraph than I could cut off my right hand. It is the voice of the story. While I've revised it, I did not change its point of view or purpose. I hear it like the voiceover at the beginning of a movie.

Discouraged, I'd put 'A Place Called Beautiful' away for long periods of time. But it called to me, and I continued submitting. Its publication in *Flyover Country* and its inclusion in this anthology reinforce what I've always believed: you don't quit on the writing you love.

MARK L. KEATS was born in Korea and raised in Maryland. He has an MFA in Creative Writing from the University of Maryland and a PhD in Literature and Creative Writing from Texas Tech University. He has received fellowships from Kundiman, The Martha's Vineyard Institute of Creative Writing, and Artist Trust.

The story began from research for a novel project that deals with the effects of war on Korea, its people, and the diaspora. I learned about a historical footnote to the Korean War, which concerned Operation Insomnia. This is where the United States bombed Pyongyang for ninety days and ninety nights straight. (Note: this is the webpage I found and learned about the operation: https://www.versobooks.com/blogs/3875-ending-the-korean-war-a-transnational-dialogue). I did my best to imagine what it was like on the other side, specifically to imagine the perspective of the Koreans who were trying to exist amidst such a traumatic timeframe: WWII, the occupation by Japan, and the civil war. Additionally, I was wondering about the tension between being helped by the same country that caused the trauma. The title is meant to be facetious because it is not uncommon for Koreans and other immigrants I've met to discuss these kinds of pasts as if it's not that big of a deal—just something they had to do.

◂

LAURA LEE LUCAS (she/her) is a VONA/Voices fellow and a member of the Horror Writers Association. Her fiction has appeared in *The Ghastling, Graffiti, Bards and Sages Quarterly, Supernatural Tales, Rigorous, Beat the Dust, Falling Star Magazine*, and *The Two Hour Transport Anthology* 2019.

There's something about being in love that makes everything else go slightly out of focus. Small pieces of your life, your hobbies, your habits, are adjusted to accommodate your lover's preferences, or their schedule. Maybe you just want to keep the peace. Maybe there's something they are really excited about, and you were planning to spend that time doing another activity, but you think to yourself 'how long has it been since I did x? is it even that important to me anyway? what if I'm just not as into it as I once was?' and you let it go to do your partner's thing. And it's not a behavior that's limited to one gender or the other.

How crucial are those parts of ourselves we let fall? Have we outgrown them, or lost them? What happens when you look around and start to wonder what exactly you have left? This is the train of thought that kickstarted 'Sargasso.' I wrote most of the story in one sitting, then left it to percolate for over a year without touching it—much like those little things (or are they?) mentioned above. It took me four tries to get the ending right. We don't always get the satisfaction of closure in real life, nor do we always get what we desire. In the end, we walk away with what we have, and nothing else.

JENNIFER MORALES is a poet, fiction writer, and performance artist whose work deals with questions of gender, identity, complicity, and harm. A Beloit College graduate (1991, Modern Languages and Literatures), Jennifer received their MFA in Creative Writing from Antioch University-Los Angeles in 2011. They served for eight years as an elected member of the Milwaukee Public School board, the first Latinx person to hold that position, and in posts in education research, fundraising, and publishing. Morales is a member of the board of the Driftless Writing Center, based in Viroqua, Wisconsin.

Meet Me Halfway (U of Wisconsin Press, 2015), their collection of short stories about life in one of the nation's most segregated cities, was Wisconsin Center for the Book's 2016 Book of the Year. Booklist called *Meet Me Halfway* 'a candid and powerful book,' and Chicago Book Review deemed it 'truly masterful' and told with a 'thorough fearlessness,' ranking it one of the Best Books of 2015. The book was a finalist for the Midwest Book Award, won an Outstanding Achievement Award from the Wisconsin Library Association, and was part of the inaugural LGBTQ Writers in the Schools program in the New York City Public Schools, among other honors.

In 2014, after more than two decades in the big-little city of Milwaukee, I moved to a trailer park in rural southwestern Wisconsin. I had lived a full life in the city: raised my kids and others' children, served in elected and appointed positions, taught Sunday school, kept my heart and hands in community struggles, and wrote a book of fiction about the place, one of the most segregated places in the nation (*Meet Me Halfway: Milwaukee Stories*).

Once I had an empty nest, I was ready for quiet, for lush greenness, a giant garden, maybe some goats. The trailer park was a relatively inexpensive way to relocate to the country while I figured out a longer-term plan. After a few years there, I couldn't help but start writing my new neighbors into a fresh batch of stories. I became particularly interested in the nature of rural masculinity and how men in the small-town Midwest are asked to tamp down philosophical inquiry, play, and tenderness, things Dan wants to pursue in 'Wiseacres.'

As a rural transplant, comparisons of life 'here' and 'there' are perhaps inevitable for me. Is the city better? Is the country? I don't think I'm spoiling the story by saying that Dan thinks for a moment that the city has an answer he's seeking, but he comes to realize the information he needs isn't attached to a particular place—it can be found inside himself.

I'm a sometime performance artist and I loved sending up this weird corner of the arts world through this story. Sometimes our work is more 'performance' than it first seems: The artist is often going through a performance to figure something out, perhaps, like the artist in this story, pretending to know something they don't yet have in their grasp.

⬤

Chicana Feminist and former Rodeo Queen, **Tisha Marie Reichle-Aguilera** (she/her) writes so the desert landscape of her childhood can be heard as loudly as the urban chaos of her adulthood. She is obsessed with food. Her stories have been anthologized in *Made in L.A. Volume 4*, *Ramblings & Reflections: SouthWest Writers Winning Words Anthology*, *GATHERING: A Women Who Submit Anthology*, and *Puro Chicanx Writers of the 21st Century*. Her flash fiction has been included in Best Small Fictions 2022. A former high school teacher, she earned an MFA at Antioch University Los Angeles and is an Annenberg Fellow at the University of Southern California. She is a Macondista, creates drama with Center Theater Group Writers' Workshop, and works for literary equity through Women Who Submit.

This story reflects the love of flowers and aversion to motherhood that my maternal grandmother had. She passed away when I was almost nine, so I have only a few memories of Gramita's fierce personality. To learn more about her, I interviewed mis, Tías, my Nina, and my Mom; they all offered very different perspectives. It's like Gramita didn't want anyone to really know who she was. So I fictionalized the information I gathered, kept the timeline of her life the same, and wrote stories that eventually became a novel, which I am submitting to independent presses. The story is set in Holtville, California—a farming community known as the Carrot Capitol of the World in the Imperial Valley near the US-Mexico border—where I spent the early years of my life. I infused Gramita's character, Isabel, with a desire to travel, to be anywhere but where she felt trapped by her life. A dream that could never be reality as long as she kept having children. This story is to honor her and all rural women who couldn't realize their dreams.

JEANETTE WEASKUS is an enrolled Nez Perce tribal member and Pushcart Prize nominee who resides on the reservation in Idaho. Her work has appeared in *Raven Chronicles*, *Yellow Medicine Review*, and *Jelly Bucket*. She enjoys traveling and spending time with family and friends.

'The Stone Frog' was written for the *Alternating Currents, Remapping Wonderland* anthology in which BIPOC writers retold classic European fairy tales within the contexts of their own cultures. The challenge in writing such a piece is to not only recreate the fairy tale using the figures and history of ones' culture but to also make it recognizable to the reader who is familiar with the original European version.

My fairy tale is the Indigenous version of 'The Metal Pig,' in which Hans Christian Anderson describes a bronze pig fountain in Florence, Italy, that was frequented by the town boys. One such lad grew into a historical Renaissance artist whose works are globally recognized. In using this framework for my tale, I chose Chief Joseph to be the historical icon from my culture and had him closely follow the adventure of the young artist who rode the pig one night when it came to life. The story implies that the artists' fame and wealth were a by-product of that magical pig ride so I worked that angle as well into this retelling.

ERIKA T. WURTH's literary-horror novel, *White Horse*, is with Flatiron/Macmillan and is an indie next pick. Her work has appeared or is forthcoming in numerous journals including *Buzzfeed*, *Boulevard*, *Lithub*, *The Writer's Chronicle*, and *The Kenyon Review*. She is a Kenyon and Sewanee fellow, and a narrative artist for the Meow Wolf Denver installation. She is represented by Rebecca Friedman (books) and Dana Spector, CAA (film). She is an urban Native of Apache/Chickasaw/Cherokee descent and was raised outside of Denver, where she lives with her partner, her two stepchildren, and her extremely fluffy dogs.

> 'When Kari Floats Down' is in some ways based off a man I knew in my twenties—I combined him with personalities from back home (Idaho Springs, Colorado, where I went to school), imagining a very middle class, Native personality who just could not get over a heartbreak from his teens—to the point where it poisons his entire life. I've always been interested in dark inner landscapes, and I hoped to layer this story in such a way as to show the contrast of his inner life with his outer—and the fact that this spiritual disjuncture eventually ends up with an inevitable irruption.

ACKNOWLEDGMENTS

"The Lesser Light of Dying Stars" by Jinwoo Chong. First published in *Salamander*, 51. Copyright © 2021 by Jinwoo Chong. Reprinted by permission of Jinwoo Chong.

"White Bird" by Risë Kevalshar Collins. First published in *North American Review*, 307.1. Copyright © 2022 by Risë Kevalshar Collins. Reprinted by permission of Risë Kevalshar Collins.

"Like None Other" by Jamie Figueroa. First published in *Agni*, 93. Copyright © 2021 by Jamie Figueroa. Reprinted by permission of Jamie Figueroa.

"Mercury Was There" by Libby Flores. First published in *Gagosian*, Summer 2021. Copyright © 2021 by Libby Flores. Reprinted by permission of Libby Flores.

"A Place Called Beautiful" by Jane Hammons. First published in *Flyover Country Magazine*, October 2021. Copyright © 2021 by Jane Hammons. Reprinted by permission of Jane Hammons.

"The Unremarkable Life of Mrs. Shin" by Mark L. Keats. First published in *museum of americana*, 23. Copyright © 2021 by Mark L. Keats. Reprinted by permission of Mark L. Keats.

Explore more short fiction published by

EASTOVER
— PRESS —
www.EastOverPress.com

You Have Reached Your Destination
Louise Marburg

"Marburg's characters find themselves in lives they
don't quite recognize, searching for signposts that can
lead them forward or tell them who they are...
These characters are as quirky as they are full of heart."
—*The New York Times*

❧

All the Rivers Flow into the Sea & Other Stories
Khanh Ha

From Vietnam to America, this collection, jewel-like,
evocative, and layered, brings to readers a unique sense of
love and passion alongside tragedy and darker themes of peril.

❧

The Cutleaf Reader
multiple volumes
Contributors to *Cutleaf*

Our annual print anthologies collect works by numerous
writers published in *Cutleaf*, our literary journal of
short stories, essays, and poetry.
(www.CutleafJournal.com)

CPSIA information can be obtained
at www.ICGtesting.com
Printed in the USA
LVHW030416220323
742167LV00004B/570